Skyward Ventures: Exploring the World of Drones

A Comprehensive Handbook for Aerial Hobbyists and Entrepreneurs

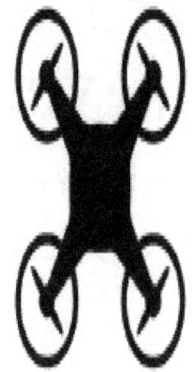

INTRODUCTION

The world moves fast. Five years ago, if you flew your drone in public, people would stop and stare, wondering if you were some kind of international spy. But that was five years ago. Things have changed quite a bit since then.

The DJI Phantom was, for the most part, the first consumer multirotor drone marketed as 'ready to fly' out of the box. It came out in 2013. At that time, about 5,000 units were sold per month. Today, that number is closer to 150,000, meaning sales grew by an incredible 3,000% over a few years. There are no signs of a slowdown, either. For the 2015 holiday season alone, over a million drones flew off the shelves (hooray, our first drone pun!).

If that isn't enough to get you excited, consider this: Consumer interest is just *half* the story.

Businesses are experimenting, too. DHL has successfully delivered packages with drones in Germany. Walmart is using drones to move goods around their warehouses. Airlines are using drones for visual inspections in Europe. The next evolution of the industrial revolution is underway!

If you're reading this book, we assume you're interested in drones and curious about how you might use them to improve your business, or start a new one. Good move. You're just in time to ride the wave of the next technological revolution.

WHY SO MUCH GROWTH?

When we first got into this business, we thought there were about three hundred different uses for drones. We now realize our estimate was low, by an order of magnitude. So, why exactly are we seeing so much growth in the industry? Let's look at a few of the major factors.

Lighter, Smaller, Smarter

For a long time, drones and their related equipment were extremely large, heavy, and expensive. The first drones, used by the military in 1955, included mounted cameras the size of a beach ball. Today, that same camera is far more powerful, and it's smaller than a golf ball.

Drones are also smarter. In earlier versions of model aircraft, your vehicle would crash as soon as you let off the sticks. But with a modern-day drone, it'll stop in place and hover perfectly still, even in the wind. With that single development alone, drones are far less intimidating than traditional model aircraft, and therefore far more appealing to the average consumer.

Hobbyists Are Fueling the Fire

Social sharing has become an obsession for some, and drones augment the experience. (Taking a selfie with a drone is way more impressive than taking a photo from the ground! We call it a "dronie.") Drones also create compelling content from the viewer's perspective. Watching a drone video is like experiencing life without gravity. It can be addicting, which is why so many drone-produced videos go viral on social media services such as Facebook and Twitter.

Drones Are a Platform

A grocery store is a platform for food. Have you ever thought about it that way? It's a system that allows food to be organized and distributed to consumers. Cell phones have become platforms, too. A mobile phone isn't just a device for talking to another person. It's actually a container for all types of software. And that software can be carried along with you in your pocket. That's what makes it so powerful.

Drones are also now a platform. A drone can be outfitted with various hardware and connected to various software. Those tools can then be launched into the sky, which creates a whole new set of applications. The technology of the drone itself isn't all that special. It's the *combination* of hardware, software, and flight that makes drones so exciting.

THERE'S A DRONE FOR THAT

Combining hardware, software, and flight allows us to solve old problems in new ways. We'll give more examples later, but here are a few to get started.

Information Gathering

A local heating and cooling company recently reached out to us because they needed to get the serial number from an AC unit installed on a roof. Instead of asking an employee or contractor to climb up a ladder to get the information, they asked us to fly our drone up to the unit and take a high-definition photo. It saved time and money, while also preventing any possibility of injury.

Cell Phone Tower Inspection

Instead of using a truck with a cherry picker to inspect a cell tower, one can use a drone that takes photos to achieve the same result. In the past, this standard inspection traditionally required multiple workers and considerable man hours. Now it can be done with a single person in minutes.

Precision Agriculture

There are a number of applications related to farming. For example, farmers can use drones to figure out exactly where their cattle are located at any given moment in time.

Drones can also improve the efficiency of crop dusting. When planes drop fertilizer or other materials on a field of crops, about 75% of the material gets blown away in the propeller wash, or "prop wash." With drones, the prop wash is pushed directly downward, since the propellers are parallel to the ground, like a helicopter. The result? No material is wasted, which translates into huge savings.

Also, farmers can use drones to determine if certain plants are showing early signs of disease. With unbelievable precision, a drone can scan for levels of nitrogen, carbon, phosphorous, and so on.

Finding a Needle in a Haystack

Let's say a young couple was honeymooning in the Caribbean, and the wife lost her turquoise ring in the sand. We could use a drone with a *hyperspectral sensor* to find it.

The sensor is able to detect minerals and compounds that give off a specific reflectivity. Knowing there's likely no other turquoise lying around on the beach, we'd take photos with the hyperspectral camera and then convert those images to black and white. The physical properties of the turquoise would appear bright white, while everything else would appear black. In other words, we'd be able to find a needle in a haystack!

DRONES ARE FOR FUN

The business and practical applications for drones are endless, but the majority of drone pilots these days are using them for recreation. And there's nothing wrong with that. Here are three examples.

FPV Racing

One of the most popular drone-related activities we've observed is FPV (first-person view) racing. With FPV racing, you're looking at a screen that's live-streaming footage from a camera attached to a drone. You then control the drone and race it through custom-designed race courses. Essentially, you're seeing through the drone's eyes as you race.

FPV racing has grown in popularity because of the speed, difficulty, and accessibility of the sport. Watching a pilot throttle his drone through a narrow tunnel at 80 miles per hour turns out to be highly entertaining.

From the pilot's perspective, it's a feasible hobby. You can get an FPV drone for a few hundred bucks, and if you're talented (or your competition sucks), you might even make your money back pretty quickly!

Photography

Drones can take photographs from vantage points you otherwise wouldn't be able to reach. Naturally, photographers are beginning to experiment with the technology. With cheaper models coming out practically every month, using a drone as an accessory is doable for both hobbyists and professionals.

Videography

The natural extension to photography is videography. We'll see more examples of this later, but videography has a host of applications, both recreational and commercial. For recreational use, drones are replacing camcorders. Instead of filming a barbeque or a birthday party from the ground, why not capture footage of the entire event from above?

Amateur filmmakers are also experimenting with drones. In many cases, footage from a drone can match the quality of a Hollywood-produced film.

WE'VE COME A LONG WAY, BUT WE'RE STILL AT THE BEGINNING

While the drone industry has progressed incredibly quickly over the past five years, we're still in the very early stages of its development as a whole.

Drone usage is growing at a much faster rate than the Federal Aviation Administration (FAA) ever could have predicted, and now they're playing catch-up. The FAA defines a drone as an aircraft. That means a drone pilot is supposed to get the same certifications as a pilot flying a 747 aircraft. We think that's a little silly, and the majority of drone pilots tend to agree. This aircraft label wasn't further defined until August 2016, when the new drone regulations became law.

Model aircraft have actually been around longer than the FAA itself. In 1981, the FAA released the Advisory Circular (AC) 9157, which is a document that basically says, "Anyone flying a model aircraft can do so if they meet the community guidelines set forth by the AMA (Academy of Modern Aeronautics)." So, is a drone a model aircraft or an *actual* aircraft? We believe it's neither. We think drones are a new category completely. Unfortunately, we don't get to make the rules.

At the time of this writing, there are no concrete privacy laws specific to drones either. The only privacy-related law appears in the federal case *Causby vs. the United States*. The case involved a chicken farmer who believed he deserved compensation because the Army violated the usable airspace of his property. The military flew aircraft too close to his property, causing his chickens to spontaneously die. The ruling stated that if you fly too low (below 500–1000 feet) over private property, the property owner might be entitled to compensation. In this case, he was entitled to compensation because the Army violated the usable airspace of his property. Yes, it's a hazy rule. And it doesn't really have to do with privacy. It's more about property.

We're giving you this background so you understand the current state of the industry. We have to be careful with terms like *rules* and *laws*. When we say *law*, we mean it went through Congress, the Senate, and the president's desk. The FAA has released a handful of rules, but there's no legal backing to those rules. In the United States, there were actually *zero laws* concerning drones until 2016. Don't worry, we'll explain this further in later chapters.

The rest of the world has been using drones commercially for decades. Companies in New Zealand, Australia, Canada, South America, and Japan are using them to solve serious issues, such as responding to heart attacks. The average time for an ambulance to deploy and arrive on-site is about nine minutes in most neighborhoods. When someone has a heart attack, they have approximately two minutes to survive. You can see how that's a problem. But within a five-mile radius, a drone can fly to a specified location within *ninety seconds*. So, a health and humanitarian group out of Europe put a defibrillator on a Y-6, which is a coaxial hex copter drone, and started sending it out as a first responder, ahead of the ambulance. This is just one example of how drones are already being used overseas.

While the lack of regulation in the United States has hampered businesses from becoming drone-friendly, history was forever changed in August 2016. The NPRM 107 (National Proposed Rulemaking 107) became a law, also known as *14 CFR 107* or "Part 107." The law negates the requirement of a private pilot's license, and it permits anyone to fly drones commercially as long as they've passed a written test. In other words, the barrier to entry just got a lot lower.

What does this mean for you? It means drones will be woven more deeply into the fabric of our society. We expect a massive influx of drone-related businesses (and drone pilots in general) over the next few years. Inevitably, a good portion of those businesses will eventually go away because of either acquisition or bankruptcy. One of our goals with this book is to ensure you're in the acquired/profitable group.

OPPORTUNITIES GALORE

Drones present so many opportunities that it's nearly impossible to list them all. We've already covered a few, but here are some other areas where we see drones having a big impact.

Real Estate

Using drones, real-estate agents can offer a more comprehensive and engaging viewing experience to excite potential home buyers. The drone can fly through the home to give a beautiful, uninterrupted tour in a single shot. Footage of the surrounding neighborhood can also add to the charm.

Any Company That Deals with Towers, Roofing, or Things in the Air

We've already talked about roofing companies. Power-line companies are another example. Typically, they pay thousands of dollars for helicopters to fly along their lines to check for issues. With drones, the bulk of that cost can be eliminated.

Wedding Videographers, or Film in General

Anything involving film is a huge opportunity. We like the example of a wedding videographer. Imagine a wedding on the coast. The drone flies in from the ocean, panning across the shoreline, and eventually zooms in on a small gathering of people at the edge of the water. How much more special and magical will those memories be through the lens of movie-grade cinematography? If you're a wedding videographer and you show a prospective client some footage like the scene we just described, we have a feeling you'll land the gig![1]

Construction

A construction crew can use a drone to map out their site and measure exactly how much material they need to remove in order to lay the foundation of a house. Then the drone can systematically take pictures to show progress over time. Companies who offer this service typically take pictures of the site every week so investors and architects can see how the project is developing. Yes, they could take pictures from the ground, but that's not as comprehensive as a shot from above.

Drones can also volumetrically map the construction site to measure the quantities of the existing materials. This means the construction team can monitor how much sand, gravel, concrete, and so on that they've used at any given time, and then benchmark these against their initial estimates. Ultimately, it improves efficiency and results in cost savings over the life of the project.

THE STATE OF THE DRONE INDUSTRY

In the world of capitalism, everyone is looking for a competitive advantage: better pricing, operational efficiencies, marketing hacks, and so on. We're seeing a mass ascension (pun intended) of drones facilitating that edge. People are seeing dollar signs—a way to turn their toy into a tool.

But the increased interest, combined with a lack of information, education, and regulation, is creating a big problem. People don't know the basic protocols, such as the fact that they need to do a pre-start-up calibration before flying. We see a lot of self-proclaimed "drone experts" out in the field, but they don't actually know what they're doing. They'll go to a site and fly in an area with rebar-reinforced concrete, completely unaware that it's likely to be scrambling their GPS signal. Then they crash. Or worse, they injure someone.

The uninformed operator says, "My drone can fly anywhere. Flying around reinforced concrete like a parking structure, and/or between two tall buildings, shouldn't be a problem." But to someone who understands radio waves and GPS signals, that's like saying, "I'm going to drive my car into the ocean." Almost everyone knows that deep standing water will cause a car to malfunction. Cars aren't designed to be driven underwater. Even in rain or snow, operating the vehicle becomes dangerous. The same is true for flying a drone between two buildings or near steel objects.

We'll learn more about this later, but here's a quick explanation: You wouldn't fly a drone between two tall buildings in GPS mode, because the GPS signals will bounce off the buildings and cause interference. This creates a margin of error in the GPS reading. The drone will then fly in the direction of the margin of error. In this case, the interference is coming from the buildings. So the drone will fly directly into the structure you're trying to avoid.

BUSINESS IS BUSINESS

If you're reading this book, we assume you're ready to start a drone business, or start using a drone to augment your current operations. With any business, there are multiple moving parts. Being a great drone pilot isn't enough. That's why our company, Drone U, is staffed with drone experts *and* business experts.

The business side of things isn't easy. If you want to run a real-estate videography business, or a production company, learning how to film great footage is only the first step. You'll then need to decide whether to outsource your editing or do it in house. And what about costs? What's your cost per battery? How often will you need to replace your equipment? How can you best market your services? What about accounting and hiring employees?

If you open a sandwich shop, you might think you'll be better off running your business independently with no outside investors or advisors. And for some people, that's fine. But the truth is that most local sandwich shops fail. The franchised shops, like Subway or Quiznos, tend to succeed. We're not saying this to discourage you. We're making an important point about operating a business. The franchises don't succeed because their sandwiches are better. They succeed because the people who run them are given a "business in a box." They're handed a proven formula that explains exactly what to do.

Through this book (and our membership site), our goal is to hand people a "business in a box" for any drone-related business. You'll learn about all the things you need to know to be a great pilot, including the proper flying techniques and how to select the right kinds of equipment. But beyond that, you'll understand all the other aspects of your business. For example, you'll learn:

- How to price your services
- How to find proper insurance
- How to draft contracts to protect yourself and your clients
- How to market your business

This book isn't just about flying drones. It's your all-in-one guide for successfully running a drone-powered business.

APPLYING YOUR DRONE TO AN EXISTING BUSINESS OR AREA OF EXPERTISE

A drone can be applied to nearly any business. But let's explore what needs to happen on a broad level. It might seem as if we're beating these points into the ground, but we can't stress them enough.

1. You have to understand the tech.
2. You have to fly well.
3. You need legal protection.
4. You must market and sell with confidence.

You Have to Understand the Tech

Knowing that drones fly and take pictures isn't enough. You need to learn how the systems actually work so you can apply them to your business and make good judgments in the field. If you don't have a solid grasp of the various sensors available, how drones operate, potential sources of interference, and so on, you'll quickly run into problems. Here's an example to demonstrate.

Let's say you're a realtor and you want to incorporate drones into your business. You decide to "learn by doing," so you buy a drone, take it out of the box, and turn it on. Well, unfortunately there was a solar flare yesterday and the KP index is seven. The drone's GPS can't connect to the satellites when the KP index is that high, so it flies away. Bye-bye drone. If you had done your homework, you wouldn't have lost your drone. You would've said, "The KP index is too high today. It's a no-fly day."

You Have to Fly Well

We'll teach you to fly, but that won't make you successful. You have to fly really *well*. Flying well requires tactical knowledge, like banking your turns in a completely smooth manner. But it's more than that. You also need to have an understanding of the regulatory information surrounding proper flight. If you're hired to film a concert, for example, you should never fly directly over the audience.

You Need Legal Protection

The FAA has historically had a hard time distinguishing between commercial and noncommercial activities (although this has changed somewhat, as we discuss in chapter 9). If you use your drone to search for a missing person and you're not earning money, that's not a commercial application. But your insurance company won't necessarily see it that way. They might say, "The FAA defines search and rescue as commercial, and you don't have the required COA (Certificate of Authorization) to fly for that purpose, so we won't cover you in the event of a crash in that case."

That would suck, right? Well, we've seen it happen. Just because you have insurance doesn't mean it's the right kind of insurance, or that it will protect you from every situation. We're here to help you avoid those kinds of common pitfalls.

You Must Market and Sell with Confidence

Let's say you're working for a boat company and you've taken some footage of their fleet of boats. Could you use that footage for another project? The answer is, "It depends." Are you selling a single license, or exclusive rights to that footage? When you're selling your work, you need to consider various pricing agreements. In this book, we'll cover all aspects of pricing, including how to price yourself competitively and handle situations like multilicensing.

WE BUILT DRONE U FOR YOU

Theory vs. Experience

Paul is one of our cofounders, chief pilot, and cohost of the *Ask Drone U* podcast. Before joining Drone U, he enrolled at another program to learn how to fly drones. This seemed like a great idea to Paul, but it turned out to be useless. Some of the instructors owned drone stores. Others had military experience with drones. Some had used drones on a few gigs, but their primary experience was more related to selling drones—not actually flying them. Not a single instructor was actually flying drones for a living. Paul then found out that the school didn't even own a single drone.

Most of the drone schools today are teaching theory. They're not teaching based on experience. That's something we set out to change. We wanted to find people who flew drones for a living, and did it well. This isn't a hobby for us. It's what we do. The philosophy of most pilots is that you can learn by doing—in other words, trial and error. In our eyes, trial and error is not a strategy. It's insanity. We certainly believe practice makes perfect, but not without getting the proper education *beforehand*. (By the way, the learning process never stops).

Teaching based on theory (versus experience) has real-life repercussions. After countless hours of flying, we realized there's a huge gap between theory and successful operation.

Before You Take a Course, Read This

Another piece of the puzzle for us was to create an affordable system that offers unparalleled value. Currently, drone training programs are expensive. Frankly, they're too expensive. That was something we didn't like, so we set out to change it. We've created a model where people can integrate the training into their monthly budget and receive more value than from any other offering available. We regularly add training materials over time, so while the monthly cost doesn't change, the value is always increasing.

Perhaps the most overlooked problem with most drone programs is their lack of depth and experience. While they might teach you how to fly a drone, they're *still* missing a lot of critical information. For example, they don't teach you how to run a drone business. They don't teach you how to write contracts to protect yourself and your work. They don't teach you the true value of your work, and how to price it accordingly.

Luckily, you don't need to take a course to get a basic understanding of drones. You can just read this book instead. We see this as the first step. Then, if a course seems prudent, you can take that step.

A Holistic Approach

Plain and simple, there just weren't any books that holistically covered this stuff, so we decided to write one. There are books about aerial videography and photography, but they're written by people who don't own drone businesses. They don't know the nuances. If you go to YouTube, you can watch videos of people flying drones all day long. But that's not an effective substitute for learning how to fly. Nor is looking on the Internet for ways to run a drone business.

This book is comprehensive. It will teach you how to pick the right hardware and software, how to fly, and how to build a successful business around it. You'll learn the systems and routines to mitigate risk, showcase amazing stories, and bypass common mistakes. We're glad you're here. Now let's see how high we can go.

[1] We should mention that other, more expensive tools can get the same type of shots. For example, a jib can get that footage, or a crane. The difference is that a drone only costs a few hundred dollars, so it's feasible for smaller businesses and solo entrepreneurs.

THE SKY (APPEARS TO BE) THE LIMIT

HOW DO I TURN A HOBBY INTO A THRIVING BUSINESS?
If you think about it, *every* thriving business starts as a hobby. That's exactly how Paul (one of our cofounders) got into the business of flying drones professionally.

One day, he and his buddy Andrew were hanging out near an ice rink downtown, casually flying a drone in an open area nearby. A stranger on skates glided toward Paul from the ice, and anxiously called out, "Hey! Cool drone! Would you be willing to capture my marriage proposal on tape? I'd pay for it. Whatever you want to do is fine. I'd just love to get this proposal on film!"

Paul paused momentarily, and then agreed. Why not? A few minutes later, he was holding a wad of crisp, green bills. *Here's hard evidence,* he thought to himself. *People want this. This is real demand.* And then the ideas started flooding in. Paul realized drones could provide utility in *countless* situations. They could literally solve thousands of problems.

Drones have created an opportunity for new businesses to emerge in nearly every industry. Turning a hobby into a business creates responsibility, but it can also open the door for you to live the life of your dreams. If flying is your dream, you've come to the right place!

Let's be real. *Turning a hobby into a business takes relentless dedication. It's not easy.* We've been teaching people how to turn their toy into a tool for years. We've done drone-related work for hundreds of clients, and we've coached thousands of drone operators.

We like to think about this in terms of overall mentality. There are two mind-sets: the Client Mentality and the Owner Mentality. The Owner sees a problem and then immediately seeks a solution. If there isn't as solution, he creates one. The Client, on the other hand, sees a problem and then looks for someone else to solve it for him. If you want to get into the drone business, you need to adopt the Owner Mentality.

You should also remove all expectations. Drones are in their infancy. You're exploring an emerging market, which means there's risk and uncertainty. Finally, you need to be willing to learn.

If you want to turn your hobby into a legitimate business, you need to set your priorities. Here's our approach:

1. *Priority One*: Make sure you have the appropriate mind-set. (i.e., the attitude of an Owner, not a Client).
2. *Priority Two*: Learn to fly well. Without that skill, you have no service to offer. This step also involves studying the mechanics, theory, and regulations related to flying.
3. *Priority Three*: Learn how to run your business effectively.

This book addresses all three priorities.

Although drones have been around for decades, it's a relatively new industry from a commercial perspective, especially here in the United States. As we mentioned in the introduction, we saw a big breakthrough in 2012 when DJI (Da-Jiang Innovations Science and Technology Company—one of the largest manufacturers of drones) released the Phantom 1. After its release, drones became more mainstream, for two main reasons:

1. The affordable price (less than $1,000)
2. The ease of learning to fly

Learning to fly a drone is a lot like skiing. Initially it's very easy, but it's hard to master. The Phantom 1 is a great way for beginners to get their feet wet without investing several thousand dollars.

As of this writing, it's estimated that DJI sells 35,000 drones a week in the United States alone, and that number appears to be increasing. The proliferation of cheaper drones has essentially created a race to the bottom. Prices are dropping rapidly, and we're now seeing drones as cheap as $50.[1] In other words, it's very affordable to buy a drone and see what all the fuss is about.

Higher-cost drone services are also decreasing. In the past, if you wanted to record aerial footage for a movie, you'd be spending $8,000–$10,000 per day, at a minimum. Today, you can film on set with a prosumer-grade drone for about $3,500 and get the same quality footage that was being recorded from big, heavy-lift copters three years ago. Why is this? It comes down to the controllability of the drone. The fluidity of shots is far better than it used to be.[2]

IT SEEMS AS IF EVERYONE HAS A DRONE—HOW HARD CAN THIS BE?
This is both an exciting time and a challenging time. You don't know what you don't know, which is why we're so glad you're reading this book. We've heard endless stories about people who've made horrible mistakes, simply because they didn't take the time to understand how drones operate on a basic level.

There's a steep learning curve from casual "dronie" to drone professional. While we've seen a proliferation of photographers and other business people getting into drones, one of two things typically happens. They either educate themselves and continue honing their skills, or they crash and say, "I'm going to stop flying." In other words, they either do their homework, or they get frustrated and quit.

We've identified hundreds of mistakes pilots typically make. You'll make mistakes, too, and you'll certainly crash. (Everyone crashes.) But if you stay informed, you'll know how to improve and grow. We'll highlight various pitfalls throughout the book, but here are a few of the usual suspects.

Calibrations, Compass, and IMU
You need to do an IMU (Inertial Measurement Unit) and "compass calibration" any time you buy a new drone or do a firmware update. If you do a firmware update and don't do an IMU calibration or a compass calibration, you're more likely to have a flyaway.

Your cell phone can cause a related problem with calibration, too. If you're trying to do a calibration with your cell phone in your pocket, and you lock in the wrong GPS coordinates because your phone interferes with the reading, you could have a flyaway upon takeoff.

Ignoring External Conditions
A lot of people think batteries have a consistent charge duration. That's false. Your battery will use more juice in various scenarios, depending on the conditions. For example, a battery that normally lasts twenty minutes might only last three to four minutes if it's thirty degrees outside. This relates to the general condition of your hardware, too. For example, propellers only last for about ten to twelve hours. If you continue flying after that, you're asking for a crash.

Orientation Confusion
If your drone takes off and the camera is facing the same direction your eyes are facing, you and the drone both have the same orientation. More specifically, if you roll right with your controller, the drone will roll to the right. And if you roll left, the drone will roll to the left. But if you turn the drone 180 degrees around so the camera is facing you, the controls become inverted. Now if you roll right, the drone will move left, and vice versa. Mastering the different orientations takes hours of practice.

Lack of Spatial Awareness
We have a buddy who tells anyone who buys a drone: "Don't fly near stuff." As overly simplistic as that sounds, it's actually great advice. If you fly a drone right out of your backyard, the chances of hitting something are quite high. If you go into a big open field and learn how to control the drone, bank your turns, get acclimated with changing orientation, and fly purely by line of sight, you'll have a much easier time improving your skills without crashing into stuff.

Almost every person who buys a drone makes one of the above mistakes. We've seen this with hundreds of students who come through Drone U, which is why we cover these issues in our *Don't Crash Course*. Just by reading this far, you've avoided 30% of the mistakes you would have made otherwise. Well done!

You might be noticing a theme here: *Education is paramount.* And that's why we've written this book. If you keep reading, or decide to take one of our courses, it will transform you into a confident pilot who can avoid common mistakes, fly safely, and cite basic laws and regulatory information to back yourself up. That confidence is priceless. It will make all the difference in allowing you to thrive as a drone operator and business owner.

SOME EXAMPLES OF HOW DRONES ARE BEING USED TODAY

Yes, there are dangers and pitfalls if you decide to start flying drones. But there are also endless opportunities. We've counted 200 industries and 300 different business types within which drones can be beneficial to your work. We touched on some cases already, but here are a few more to sprinkle into the mix. We hope these examples give you ideas about how you might be able to incorporate drones into your own workflows.

Roof Inspections

We've seen roofing companies use drones for roof and interior inspections. They use radiometric thermal cameras, which allow them to see temperature deviations in the roof line. A temperature deviation signals a crack in the foundation of the walls or holes in the roof. Using the camera to investigate further, they can then tell if it's leaking, where the leak is located, the severity of the leak, and whether or not there's mold. Without a drone, they'd need to rip down walls, and even remove the roofing entirely in some cases. With a drone, however, they can get the job done in minutes, with zero demolition or excavation required, and practically zero liability. It saves time, not to mention thousands of dollars.

One other application relating to roof inspections that many do not know or think about, but that can literally save lives (not just time and money), is for fire departments. During a structure fire, the ability to put a drone in the air to see hot spots on the roof can help firefighters know where to penetrate the roof and fight the fire more effectively. This is just one of the many applications and benefits that could be realized in regard to public safety departments.

LIDAR

LIDAR is a powerful scanning tool that uses lasers to distinguish objects, people, plants, and pretty much anything in our environment. It's how self-driving cars are able to identify the streets so they know where to drive. LIDAR can also see through pipes and determine if there are cracks. It's used by the military to map out targets so they can scale-model specific areas and know where to attack. And it can be used to thwart expensive and dangerous explosions in the oil and mining industries. These are just a few of the applications.

Anything Involving Cameras and Sensors

As you can tell from these examples, there are various types of cameras. The human eye can see about 1% of all light. Thanks to cameras and sensors, we can now see about 30% of all light. Drones make these cameras mobile, and that combination gives us access to all kinds of information that would have been impossible to gather otherwise. We'll discuss LIDAR and other sensors in more depth later.

LEARNING BY DOING

Can you learn by doing? You already know the answer. If you don't understand how the various systems work, the consequences can be catastrophic. That said, you *do* need to practice flying to get better at it. Our recommendation is to take your time reading this book, get up to speed on the theory and technology, and *then* start flying.

Thousands of things can go wrong when it comes to flying drones, and the only way to advance this industry is by educating people. We need to be talking about the issues and digging deeper into the *why*. Because we've been doing this for years, we have practical experience. Sharing this knowledge will thwart crashes and help people (like you) fly successfully, enjoy the freedom of flight, and grow the industry.

Because the technology is moving at such a rapid pace, it's hard to keep up. Firmware updates (updates from the manufacturer) happen multiple times per month. And it seems like a new drone model is released every week. The whole idea behind this book, and our company, Drone U, is that we hope to create a community *by* pilots *for* pilots, so we can share practical experience and maintain a competitive advantage (not only in business, but in general knowledge pertaining to flight).

Fortunately, at Drone U, we have actual FAA certified PPL (private pilot license) pilots and certified flight instructors, and they're able to give our students information from their schooling and experience. This constant flow of information helps us learn, mitigate crashes, save lives, and maintain a competitive advantage over competitors in the industry.

Small changes over time create the most dramatic and profound effects in the long run. This is true in life and in flying drones. Understanding the foundational flight systems, and how those systems work together, will give you the best opportunity to become a great pilot. But it's important first to learn about the regulatory environment and how best to navigate it (yup, another flight pun).

---

1 As a side note, Drone U recommends buying smaller, cheaper drones before moving up in price to the consumer Phantom or solo drones. Smaller drones are tough to fly, but we think that's a good thing. You can learn to fly them in your house, which is more difficult than being outside, so it will force you to work on your precision.

2 This is due to gimbals, which we'll discuss later. Essentially it keeps the camera stable even though the drone is moving around.

TURBULENCE

FLIMSY GOVERNANCE: THE SKYPAN AND PIRKER RULINGS
Drones have become more mainstream over the past decade, but governance around the industry generally hasn't kept up. In this chapter, we'll dig into the historical flight regulations for flying drones and some recent changes. While you might have the urge to skip this section, we think it's worth your while. We've tried to keep it succinct, while still highlighting the major rules and procedures. We wish things were a little more clear, but unfortunately, there's always a bit of turbulence when you're playing in an emerging market.

In the early 1980s, the AMA was in charge of establishing regulations for model aircraft. The FAA had given them full control to create the guidelines, rules, and set of standards by which we fly. But in 2012, at the request of congress, the FAA became more involved.

Congress essentially told the FAA to create a better regulatory framework around the commercial use of drones. So they created the Section 333 Exemption form, which validates pilots to fly commercially. Unfortunately, the form acted as a catchall for every kind of pilot, including aircraft pilots. Because of this, many drone operators felt the requirements to obtain a 333 Exemption were unnecessary in the context of their work.

For example, Skypan International (a drone-centric aerial photography company) sued the FAA, essentially stating that the FAA lacked the authority to regulate drones. Consequently, the FAA slapped Skypan with a $1.9 million fine for operating without a 333 Exemption in restricted airspace without a transponder. Ultimately, Skypan applied for and acquired a 333 Exemption, at the approval of the FAA.

This isn't the only case we've seen. In 2012, Rafael Pirker was flying a drone to take aerial photos for the University of Virginia. The FAA took him to court for commercial flight and flying recklessly. In that landmark case, NTSB (National Transportation Safety Board) judge Patrick Geraghty ruled that the FAA had no authority to regulate the flight of model aircraft (simply stated). Pirker didn't get fined a dime. Then the FAA appealed the case and fined him $1,100 for reckless flight, albeit not for operating commercially.

This case set the precedent that drone operators could fly for commercial purposes without a 333 Exemption, which is why Skypan saw no fault in their behavior. So, why are we mentioning it? Because it can still come into play in the form of client suspicion. Clients often perceive the 333 Exemption as a requirement.

One of the problems we've seen with drone regulation in the United States is that other countries have fewer requirements, so international businesses are able to operate more freely, which prevents companies in the United States from staying competitive on a global scale. Most developed countries don't require a private pilot's license to fly a drone because the systems, knowledge, and skills necessary to fly an aircraft are extremely different from those necessary to fly a drone. The United States is one of the only remaining developed countries yet to use drones commercially on a large scale. Mainly, this comes down to a lack of comprehensive regulation.

THE DISCONNECT: PERCEPTION IS REALITY
A friend of ours, Bob, was asked to take photos of real estate situated near an airport. It was a charity job (not for hire). For a hobby flight such as this, Bob should be allowed to fly within five miles of the airport, as long as he establishes communication with the air traffic control (ATC) tower. Unfortunately, when Bob contacted the ATC, they told him he didn't have permission to fly. Bob tried to explain he wasn't asking for permission and didn't need it. He was simply notifying them. He even recited the applicable section of the 2012 FMRA (FAA Modernization and Reform Act), describing his rights. It didn't matter. The ATC operator wouldn't oblige.

This is a perfect demonstration of the disconnect between the FAA, FSDO (Flight Standards District Offices, which is basically for flight safety), and the drone community at large. Even after Part 107, this remains a problem because hobbyists can fly most anywhere without permission, whereas commercial operators are having difficulty obtaining airspace clearance. We are anxious to see a solution to this dilemma for the FAA so that it becomes much more efficient for the commercial pilot to gain needed permissions.

Right now, safe drone operation is really driven more by ethics and professionalism than anything else. This is something we teach at Drone U. It's common sense to some degree, but it needs to be reinforced. For example, you should never fly over someone's head. Even if it's a closed set for a Hollywood shoot and you got an FAA waiver and you got permission from the director and the participants, we still wouldn't recommend it.

WHAT CONSTITUTES GOOD ETHICS?

There is no clear agreement on what constitutes good ethics, and nobody is enforcing it. In late 2015, a drone crashed on the front lawn of the White House. It just turned out to be a drunk guy who lost control of his drone, but it caused a stir within the media. President Obama made a public statement in response to the incident, saying that drone regulations were lacking and better guidelines were necessary.

But here's the problem: We've been waiting over a decade for clear drone rules. At Drone U, we believe it's up to us, the drone community, to police ourselves.

The FAA recently published a report saying there were over eight hundred "near misses" with drones and airplanes. Then the AMA checked their own sources and concluded the number was actually twelve. To us, it doesn't matter whether the number is eight hundred or twelve. Frankly, it should be zero. Flying within five miles of an airport after getting permission from the ATC (like our friend Bob) is okay. Flying over the White House, restricted areas, or directly in the path of an airplane—not so much. Unfortunately, drone operators who make ill-advised decisions are holding the industry back for everyone else.

Will the legislative arena get more clear? Yes. In fact, it has. In 2016, a law called *14 CFR 107* passed through Congress. It requires pilots to obtain a *remote* pilot certificate, which is much different than a standard pilot's license. Now hobbyists and commercial pilots are able to obtain official documentation with far more ease.

As we've said, we expect to see up to 300% growth in drone-related businesses in 2016, and then a massive correction as companies either merge or fail. This type of growth, combined with a high frequency of regulatory updates, can be tough to navigate. Our goal at Drone U is to help people through the turbulence—to work together to gain a competitive advantage.

After reading this book, you'll feel more comfortable about where you can fly and where you shouldn't fly. But it's not just about understanding the regulatory landscape. In the next chapter, we'll learn about the actual mechanics of flight and the various types of hardware and software you might end up using.

LEARNING TO FLY SAFELY
Drones fly much differently than any other aircraft. They don't fly like planes or helicopters. They move in any direction, like a flying saucer. There are four basic movements:

1. Elevation: Up and down
2. Roll: Lateral movement from right to left
3. Pitch: Forward and backward
4. Yaw: Rotation

There is a progression of techniques to learn how to fly. You can think of it like a video game. Just like a first-person shooter or a racing game, you learn the basic controls in the first few levels. Then as you progress, you start combining different moves and using advanced techniques.

The first mistake is buying a big, expensive drone instead of starting with a smaller model. Normally, we tell our students to start with a Syma X5C drone. It only costs $50 on Amazon. You can find it just about anywhere, and you can crash it a few hundred times without breaking it. It'll save you a *lot* of money in the long run.

Learning to fly a small drone is actually more difficult than using a larger model like a Phantom or an Inspire 1. With a smaller model, your movements need to be more precise. If you learn to master a small drone, you'll have an easier time switching to a bigger model later.

Most DJI drones have elevation stability, meaning the drone will correct itself to level flight, regardless of how you move the copter. If you pitch forward, it will automatically go back to stable and level flight. You might not have hover control, but it will always be level.

The majority of drones are quadcopters, which means they have four motors, four electronic speed controllers, and a power plant.[1] If you fly a quadcopter and you lose a prop or a motor, you lose the whole vehicle.

As we've mentioned, if the camera is facing away from you, you and the drone have the same orientation. If the camera is facing toward you, the orientation is reversed. When you reverse your orientation, you reverse the roll—so if you try to roll right, you'll end up rolling left. This is one of the most common causes of crashes for beginners.

Before explaining how to fly, we want to teach you about the core mechanics of drones. In the next few sections, we'll talk about various technologies, mechanical parts, and software tools.

BASIC DRONE TECHNOLOGIES AND PARTS
Drones for Mapping
With technology evolving so rapidly in the drone world, there will surely be a wide range of UAVs (unmanned aerial vehicles) that are capable of and quite good at mapping. The most comprehensive mapping software, such as DroneDeploy for example, continues to expand their list of compatible UAV options. Mapping can be used for a number of things, such as volumetrically measuring the amount of coal that's going to be outputted from a mine and exported on a train. Up until recently, it would take a computer hours to stitch photos together to form an orthomosaic map. Now, the data can be transferred from the drone to your computer in almost real time.

Drones for Data Collection
DJI recently released the XT Gimbal. The XT Gimbal is the very first stabilized radiometric thermal camera to be released in the market. It's also the first thermal camera that can be operated and controlled from the ground via your tablet. With a thermal camera, you can search for things like missing insulation in a home.

Mechanical Parts
There are five main components to every drone:

1. Flight controller
2. Electronic speed controller
3. Battery
4. Motor

5. Propellers

Flight Controller
The flight controller is by far the most important aspect of the vehicle. It's like the drone's brain. It tells the motors how fast to spin the propellers, and it processes the data of the IMU (the gyroscopes and the GPS) to keep itself level. These built-in stabilizers are one of the main reasons so many people are now buying drones. Before this technology existed, it was almost impossible to avoid a crash. If you moved the sticks one millimeter the wrong way, you'd spin out of control. But with the controller, if you start veering off in the wrong direction, you can simply let off the sticks, and the drone will stop in place, stabilize itself, and hover until you apply pressure to the sticks again.

Electronic Speed Controller
The electronic speed controller manages how many amps (power) are going through the motor. It also controls the polarity, or direction, that the motor is spinning. This essentially acts as your accelerator and your brakes.

Battery
The battery is the drone's power source. That's relatively easy to understand. What people often fail to realize is that the battery's charge duration will change depending on the external flying conditions. For example, the 3DR Solo uses a 4S battery. Flying that drone at a low elevation will result in a longer battery endurance. Flying it at a higher elevation, such as in the mountains of Colorado, will significantly reduce the battery life. Why? Because the air is thinner, so the motor has to work much harder to get the same amount of lift. This is true for all drone batteries. We've seen drones catch fire because the battery was running too hot (more on this later).

Motor
The motor is the engine. The harder it works, the faster the propellers spin.

Propellers
The propellers are the "wings" of the drone.

Sensors and Payloads

Our friend Jason Bache has said that the innovation over the past decade basically boils down to this: "Compact sensors working together, fueled by creative software."

Some of the most common sensors include gyroscopes, compasses, microphones, cameras, GPS, NFC (near field communication), and biometric readers. The first thermal cameras were water cooled. They weighed over one hundred pounds and were transported on large aircraft. Now they're so small that they can fit on your cell phone. This means even small drones can be mounted with sensors.

Because most sensors are now augmented with software, many of them have become Internet-connected devices, which creates an entire platform and a new set of practical applications.

We're also seeing the rapid development of light-based sensors, including SWIR (short-wave infrared), LWIR (long-wave infrared), and MWIR (mid-wave infrared) technology.

Mid-wave infrared technology is very effective for identifying cancerous cells, without any invasive procedures. You can imagine a scenario in which a typical visit to a hospital would involve a preliminary diagnosis gathered from drones in the parking lot. You could have your diagnosis before walking in the door! Short-wave infrared is great for seeing through smoke, and long-wave works well for night vision. These are just a few of the applications.

Remember, your drone is a platform. So while some of this may feel overwhelming, you only need to concern yourself with the sensors that relate to your specific area of interest. The same holds true for operating software.

DRONE OPERATING SOFTWARE

Much of the software for your drone will come with your purchase. You'll be able to access it online from your computer or tablet. For example, DJI has an app called GO. At this point, most drone manufacturers have some brand-specific program intended to give access to most everything you'll need for your drone.

You can now control individual aspects of your flight through the app. For example, you may be able to adjust the speed of the gimbal, or the reaction time between your controller and your drone. These are called your expo and gain settings. You can manipulate these settings to change the performance of your drone. We've tested this. For example, we've changed the settings on a Phantom 2 and been able to reach a top speed of 75 miles per hour, when the specs say its max speed is supposed to be 25 miles per hour.

The software you'll need to learn depends on how you use your drone. For example, if you're interested in aerial videography and photography, you'll need to learn Photoshop, Final Cut Pro, and Adobe Premier. If you want to get into mapping, you'll want to look into Pix4D, or Drone2map.

CAMERA SENSORS

We'll cover sensors in more depth later, but here are the main types:

Electro Optical (EO): These are the digital cameras in our phones.
Thermal/Infrared: With infrared cameras we can see through clouds and smoke.
LIDAR: A powerful scanning tool that uses lasers to distinguish objects, people, plants, and pretty much anything in our environment.
Multispectral: Multispectral sensors really are great for looking at plant health, water quality assessment, vegetation index, and plant counting.
Hyperspectral: These can identify specific bands of light.

BATTERIES

Your cell phone uses a lithium *ion* battery. Your drone uses a lithium *polymer* battery. There's a big difference. A lithium ion battery is a very stable battery. It's very safe in your pocket. A lithium polymer battery allows for a much deeper charge and a much faster discharge than a lithium ion battery, but it's significantly more dangerous.

If you don't properly charge and discharge your drone's battery, it will literally light on fire. There have been news reports of hoverboards around the country sporadically catching fire. That's because they're not being cared for properly. When a lithium polymer battery touches oxygen, it spontaneously combusts. It creates a massive fire, which can only be put out with a chemical solvent. It can't be put out with water.

In the past, we would charge these batteries like we fill up our gas tanks. When you fill up your gas tank, you go to the station, pump your gas as quickly as possible until it turns off, and then top it off. That's exactly what a balance charge does to a lithium polymer battery.

Higher-end drones have balance circuits that automatically charge your battery properly. You plug it into the wall, and the balance charge will be perfect. On cheaper drones, you won't necessarily have that functionality, so the batteries will tend to puff if they become overly discharged. When a battery begins to puff and expand, it's more susceptible to combustion and should be disposed.

Here are some things to keep in mind when charging or handling batteries:

1. When you fly with batteries on an airplane, you should never, ever check luggage with batteries in them. (This is actually a federal regulation at most airports these days). You should always carry on your batteries, even if you're flying with your drone. You can check the drone, but make sure to carry on the batteries.
2. Discharge the batteries to about 60% to either store them or travel with them.
3. The battery should be kept in some sort of container so that the leads cannot touch each other and create a spark (also known as a *LiPo fire*).
4. After every ten flight sessions, you should do a deep cycle charge.

Here's how to do a deep cycle charge:

1. Fly the drone around until your battery is at about 3.6 volts loaded. (*Loaded* means all the motors are spinning, the camera is on, the drone is on, and it's airborne.)
2. Bring it down to the ground with the motor still spinning.
3. Wait for each battery cell to get down to 3.3 volts. At that point, the battery is at its lowest safe level of depletion.
4. Shut down your drone, and put the battery on your charger to get a full charge.

Common Problems and Errors Involving Batteries

1. *Don't drop your battery.* It could light on fire if you drop it.
2. *Don't leave your battery unattended when it's charging.* It could light on fire without warning. If that happens, you want to be present so you can put out the fire as quickly as possible. (This is rare, but it can happen, especially if you have an older battery and it was overly discharged.)
3. *Don't fly for too long,* especially in extreme weather conditions or at high altitudes. Remember, your battery is working harder at higher altitudes, so it won't last as long.

You might fly for fifteen to twenty minutes in the summertime, but if you go out on a cold day in January, you'll likely get a critical battery warning after a few minutes. If you're wondering what happened, it's due to the temperature. We tell all our students to keep their batteries warmed up until the exact moment they're ready to fly. We even tell people to put thermal insulators around their batteries to keep them warm in flight. The warmer the battery on a cold day, the longer it will last. People make this mistake during the holidays all the time. They get a drone for Christmas. They don't understand that the battery is only going to last 50% to 60% of the advertised time, so it runs out of juice and they crash.

ONE-OPERATOR VS. TWO-OPERATOR SYSTEMS
In a single-operator scenario, you're controlling the vehicle and the camera. In a dual-operator system, one person controls the drone and the other person controls the camera.

When you're first learning to fly, you should fly as a single operator. This will force you to learn the craft inside and out. You'll learn how to control the gimbal and camera while you're in flight, and you'll gain a better understanding of the relationship between the camera's orientation and the drone's orientation.

As you get into more professional situations, you might find that a dual operator setup is required. For example, if you're working on a movie, you'll normally have one person flying the drone and one person flying the camera. The person flying the drone would typically have his or her own dedicated FPV theater.

As the FAA law continues to be refined and (most likely) added to, you may someday need two people whenever you fly commercially, regardless of the project. There may be a requirement to always have a "visual observer" who essentially watches and ensures you don't hit anything. We hope this does not come to be the case, however. This would very much be overkill in most commercial applications. Stay tuned...

SAFE FLIGHT CONTROLS

As we've discussed, *pitch* is forward and backward motion, *roll* is lateral motion from side to side, *yaw* is your rotation, and *elevation* is up and down motion.

Most new pilots pick a point, take off, fly to that point, and then turn the drone around and fly to the next point. The good pilots are the ones who bank their turns. They're the people who say, "Okay, here's point A, and here's point B. Not only am I going to roll; I'm going to pitch forward, roll, and begin my yaw." You can always tell a good pilot by how much yaw they use, whether that's with the airline industry, powered parachutes, or drones. How much yaw you use, and the smoothness and fluidity in which you can do it, defines your level of skill.

How do you get better at this? It's very simple: *Practice.*

We have an exercise at Drone U called a box drill. We essentially map out a square in the sky. You then fly your drone from point to point on the box.

After box drills, we then have you change your orientation. You flip the drone around and do the exact same movements. Then we move into slow-banking turns. You take that linear motion of going from point A to point B and begin curving that motion as much as possible.

When you do these more advanced motions, you begin to lose elevation. This happens in powered parachutes and planes as well. When you make a banking turn, you begin to lose elevation because you're losing surface area of the wing, which reduces lift. You have to increase your elevation when you're doing these turns to create and maintain the smoothest and most fluid flight path.

These exercises incorporate all the movements that make up any flight path: pitch, roll, yaw, and elevation.

LANDING

Landing Orientation

Whenever you land, your drone should be facing the same direction you're facing. In other words, your orientation should be the same. During a landing, you have to make microadjustments, so your reactions need to be immediate. If the orientation of your drone is backward, all of the controls are flipped, which can really screw you up.

> *Pro Tip:* "Thumbs Up." What's the one motion you should memorize if you're about to hit something? Whether it's during a landing or mid-flight, always remember: "Left thumb forward." That will result in upward elevation. If you're about to hit something, you need to elevate as quickly as possible. The higher you go, the fewer things you can hit.

How Flight Controls Mitigate Risk

To understand landing, we need to define two different flight modes that we haven't explained yet. Most drones have two (or sometimes three) essential flight modes. The two most common modes are *GPS mode* and *Attitude mode.*[2]

In GPS mode, your GPS location data is constantly being collected so your drone can calculate its exact position in space. The drone will always try its best to stay level, and it will stop in place if you let off the sticks. This is the mode we recommend for almost all situations as a beginner, *except landing.*

In Attitude mode, GPS information is not collected, and the drone will continue moving in whatever direction it was headed in before you let off the sticks. It's like a hockey puck on ice. If you hit the puck with your stick, the puck will keep gliding in the direction you hit it.

To give one more example, if you're in GPS mode and you roll right just before letting off the sticks, the drone will stop in place and begin hovering. If you're in Attitude mode and you perform the same action, the drone will continue rolling right, even after you let off the sticks. It'll slow down a little, but it won't stop.

A lot of people make the mistake of trying to land in GPS mode. It's smarter to land in Attitude mode. If you land in GPS mode, landing is more difficult because the computer will try to maintain its position and counteract the movements of the wind as you land. Those adjustments can get in the way of your landing because of the ground-wash effect. In Attitude mode, you can reach a certain level of downward elevation and then let the drone slowly glide down at that angle without worrying about any automatic recalculations from the drone itself.

Landing in the Wind

You should land into the wind (i.e., against it). If you land against the wind, it will likely pull your drone back and up. To counteract this, you can simply pitch forward. By contrast, if you land with the wind, it will push your drone forward and down. This is harder to counteract and can result in a tip-over landing. A tip-over is when your drone lands but then tips forward because of the wind, which often causes the two front propellers to break.

Avoiding Your Own Prop Wash

When flying a drone, you should never fly straight down. That's the only motion that won't work, because when you fly straight down, you'll get caught up in a *vortex rotor wash* or *vortex ring state*. This is essentially when you're flying in your own propeller wash and it sucks you in. It's almost impossible to land smoothly if you get caught up in your own wash.

Landing in Mobile Situations

Let's say you're on a boat and you're flying your drone from the boat. How do you land your drone on an object that's moving? In this scenario, we often see *catch landings*. A catch landing is when you literally catch your drone in the air.

To execute this type of landing, you would bring the drone to the bow of the boat, slowly bring the drone to arm's length, put your thumb on one side of the battery and your index and middle fingers on the other side, and grab it out of the air. Catch landings are okay for Phantoms and Solos, but for anything larger they're probably a bad idea. Enrique Iglesias lost all sensation in his fingers trying to catch his Inspire 1. Let's hope that doesn't happen to you.

When you're landing in these mobile situations, you have to match the speed of whatever you're landing on. It's possible to land on the surface of a moving vehicle. It's just much more difficult.

Remember, you should be in Attitude mode so the drone can float to you. In GPS mode, it will hover in place, which is a problem.

You should always fly in the relative direction of the vehicle's movement. So, if you were on a boat and facing forward off the bow, the drone should be facing forward off the bow, too. You would then do a small reverse pitch to match the speed of the boat, and slowly decrease it until you could either catch the drone or land it. It might be difficult to picture this, but once you do it in practice, you'll get a better understanding for how it works.

THE BASIC WORKFLOW FOR GETTING READY TO FLY

1. *Do a pre-flight inspection.*
    1. Make sure you don't have more than ten hours on any of your props. After even ten hours of flight time, you should replace them.
    2. Make sure all the screws are tight.
    3. Make sure there's no interference between the drone and the remote. Things that can cause interference include Wi-Fi routers, power lines, microwaves, and your cell phone. Staying at least ten feet away from any such device will put you in the clear. Leave your phone in your car or at home.
    4. Do a compass calibration whenever you move thirty miles or more from your previous flight. (Don't do a compass calibration next to anything made of steel. It can scramble the calibration.)
    5. You should be at least twenty-five feet from any massive metal objects, such as a car.
    6. Stay away from reinforced concrete, such as a parking structure.
    7. Make sure no one is within fifty feet of the drone.
2. *Turn on your remote.* It's important to do this before turning on your drone. The remote should also be the last thing you turn off when you land (after turning off the drone). When your drone takes off, the remote knows the drone's starting location. When the drone lands, the remote will note its landing position. If you turn off the remote before the drone, it will lose the signal to the controller. If the remote hasn't been turned on when you turn the drone on again, and the drone realizes it's not in the same place as where it last took off, it will literally take off and fly back to the "home" position. This is why it's extremely important to turn on the remote first, before you turn on the drone. This ensures the drone will establish a connection with the remote and won't try to fly to its previous location.
3. *Turn on your drone.*
4. *Perform an IMU calibration.* You won't find this in the Section 333 Exemption form. You need to do this as soon as you unpack your new drone, and you should also do it whenever you do a firmware upgrade. If you don't perform this step, your chances of a flyaway increase.
5. *Record your home point position.* If you don't record your home point position and you lose the transmission signal from the remote to the drone, the drone will lose its home point position and you'll have a flyaway. On the DJI drone, you'll know that the home point position is recorded when you see a strobing green line.
6. *Wait for a GPS lock.* Your GPS lock comes with home point position. Once you get your home point position and GPS lock, you're ready to take off.

We recommend learning to fly in a big open field (i.e., not near stuff!). In the next chapter, we'll discuss how to fly *well*.

---

1 There are also hexacopters (six propellers) and octocopters (eight propellers). What's the benefit of that? You get a heavier payload, you can fly much larger cameras, and there are more points of redundancy if one of your props fails.
2 3D Robotics defines these modes as *GPS mode* and *Manual mode*. Yuneec calls them *Smart mode* and *Angle mode*. They're all the same thing.

Flying a drone is unlike flying any other aircraft, mainly because you can move in any direction. As we've explained, the only direction you should avoid is straight down. Most drones under $300 don't have stabilization functionality, meaning there's no gyroscope to keep them level. You simply control the elevation, roll, pitch, and yaw.

    We tell our students to start with a cheaper drone, like the Syma X5C (which sells for around $50), because it's more difficult to fly. It's only five inches wide, and you can crash it over and over again without a problem. Without relying on a gyroscope to balance you out, you'll become a better pilot. Then when you move up to the bigger drones, you'll have the confidence and skill to fly well.

When we train a new student, we start off with GPS mode for a few hours, but then we switch to Attitude mode. We told you earlier that GPS is helpful for hovering your drone when you let off the sticks, but it's still better to learn initially with Attitude mode. It's sort of like learning to drive a manual (stick-shift) car versus an automatic. If you learn the manual mode first, you'll understand how the gears of the car work, and you'll know which gears are used for which speeds. Then when you switch to automatic, it's easier to drive because you understand the underlying mechanics. The same is true of Attitude mode versus GPS mode. It's better to start with the more difficult option so you can better handle the vehicle. Then you'll be able to switch effortlessly between the two modes as necessary.

CHOOSING A FLIGHT MODE

There are various scenarios that lend themselves to one flight mode over the other. For example, if you're into photography, you'll become very familiar with GPS mode. Why? Because GPS allows you to hover perfectly still in place. When you're trying to capture a photo, the ability to hover while you adjust your camera settings is crucial. It means you can find the perfect angle, adjust your filters, and capture a crystal-clear image.

If you're a videographer, you'll become more familiar with Attitude mode. Attitude mode will make your pans smoother. It will give you more control of the drone so you can get the exact movement you want. This flight mode is more difficult, but once you fine-tune your skills, you'll love the flexibility that Attitude mode provides. If you fly in GPS mode while trying to film video, and you let off the sticks, your drone will break to a stop, which usually ruins the shot.

FLIGHT SYSTEMS, FORMS, AND ROUTINES

We've already talked about the essential parts of a drone, but to refresh your memory, here they are again:

1. Flight controller
2. Electronic speed controller
3. Battery
4. Motor
5. Propellers

Let's talk about how they relate to each other. The relationship between the size of the propeller, the size of the electronic speed controller (ESC), and the size of the motor is important. If your propeller is too large for the motor, the motor will draw too much amperage out of the ESC. If the ESC gets too hot because it's drawing too much amperage, you'll have a fire. You'll lose the ESC, and when you lose the ESC, you lose the motor, which mean you lose the drone.

You can also think about this in terms of redundancy. As you work on riskier or larger-scale projects, you may want to upgrade to a larger drone, simply for the benefits of redundancy. People who fly drones for movies typically use octocopters or hexacopters. When you're trying to capture a shot and there's limited time and resources, you don't want to risk losing the shot because of a mechanical malfunction. With a hexacopter or octocopter, if you lose a prop or your ESC or a motor, you can still maintain the shot and then land on the ground safely to make repairs. With a quadcopter, you'd be out of commission.

Propeller Wear and Tear

The human brain is fallible. That's why we offer a pre-flight checklist (found in chapter 3). It will remind you to check your equipment, which is extremely important. For example, the average life span of a propeller for a DJI Phantom is about twenty hours of flight. It's hard to keep track of this, so it's best just to check your propellers before every flight. At around five hours of flight, the prop will begin to bend and lose its structural integrity. This is called *tracking*. When the blade bends upward, it takes more power, more draw, and more amperage from the ESC, which reduces your flight time. This again demonstrates how all the parts of your drone are related. Over time, the propeller will crack, become unbalanced, and ultimately tear or break completely.

How to Prevent a Flyaway
There are two fundamental things you have to do before you fly in order to avoid a flyaway.

1. *IMU calibration*: This ensures the drone knows how to stay level. If you have a DJI drone, you can use the GO app to do the IMU calibration. You should do this calibration whenever there's a firmware update as well.
2. *Compass calibration*: The compass calibration looks for satellites to determine the drone's location in space. Make sure you wait until your home point is identified. (This means the drone knows where it is.)

The manufacturer will say you should do a compass calibration every time you fly. You can certainly do this, but people tend to make mistakes, which causes the compass calibration to be wrong. And that can lead to a flyaway. Typical mistakes include doing a calibration while wearing an iWatch or with your phone in your pocket. Those are ferromagnetic devices, which means they emit a magnetic field that could interfere with the GPS information. For this reason, we recommend doing a compass calibration only when you're taking off from a location more than a few miles from your last takeoff area. For example, if you always go to the same field by your house to fly your drone, you don't need to do a compass calibration every time you fly. But if you drive an hour away, you should.

TYPES OF INTERFERENCE
There are various types of interference that can cause calibrations to go awry, and you need to be aware of them.

Metal: Anything made of metal can cause interference. This includes rebar reinforced concrete, so parking structures are to be avoided.

Ferromagnetic devices: These are devices with an electromagnetic field. Common culprits include your iWatch and your phone. Wi-Fi routers, CB radios, and radio towers can also cause issues. If you want a more accurate way of measuring the magnetic environment of your location, buy a *spectrum analyzer*.

As an example, if you take off near a bike rack made out of steel, your compass information could get scrambled and cause a flyaway. This is why we tell people to be at least twenty-five feet away from anything magnetic when doing a compass calibration.

TOILET BOWLING
If your drone starts moving in small circles and rolling from side to side, your drone is *toilet bowling*. Toilet bowling is a symptom of an inaccurate GPS reading. If this happens, your compass calibration is likely off, and you should immediately switch to Attitude Mode and bring your drone back to the home location to land. If you lose radio signal from your remote to the drone, and the drone doesn't have accurate GPS information, you'll experience a flyaway.

NONFATAL PROBLEMS

There are various issues that can affect your flight but that aren't completely prohibitive. For example, when you fly in the cold, your battery works harder, which reduces flight time. To mitigate this, you can heat your batteries before flying. We'll often warm up our batteries by blasting the heat in the car and setting them on the dashboard while driving to the flight location.

Barometric pressure also plays a role in how your drone flies. Your drone will operate very differently at higher altitudes. In those conditions, it has to work harder to stay airborne, which means your battery won't last as long.

Wind can cause problems as you fly, but you'll usually be able to deal with it. The wind speed you can handle will depend on your particular drone model. Bigger models can handle more wind. Smaller models won't be able to combat the wind as effectively. For the Phantom series of drones, beginners shouldn't fly if the wind speed is over 12–15 miles per hour. If you're more advanced, you can probably still fly with wind gusts up to 20–25 miles per hour. Keep in mind, if the wind is strong, the quality of your photos and videos will decrease.

Finally, you may also experience general technical difficulties. For example, your tablet won't always be fast enough to run a consistent FPV feed from the drone. The FPV app could crash, in which case you'd have no vision, but you would still be able to fly the vehicle.

HOW TO JUDGE WHETHER OR NOT YOU SHOULD FLY

You probably shouldn't fly in the following conditions:

- The wind speed is over 20 miles per hour.
- The KP index is above four.
- You don't have at least three miles of visibility.
- There's fog.
- It's raining or snowing heavily.
- The dew point and the temperature are within five degrees. (This can cause ice to build up on your propellers, send them out of balance, and induce a crash.)
- You're near large crowds of people.
- You're near moving traffic.
- You're near a helipad (such as at hospitals).
- You're near an airport.
- You're near critical infrastructure, such as dams.
- You're on private property without permission.

Generally, you shouldn't do the following:

- Fly over 400 feet.
- Fly beyond visual line of sight.
- Fly below the tree line in your neighborhood. (Don't give people any reason to think you're spying on them. An altitude of 200–300 feet is usually good.)

EFFECTIVE WAYS TO DRILL AND PRACTICE

Practice makes perfect. It's true. But you need to practice correctly. First of all, don't fly in your neighborhood or your backyard. Fly in an open field, preferably an AMA park. AMA parks are designated flying fields. A lot of municipalities have inhibited flight at other parks and recreational sites. Once you find a convenient and safe location for practice, here are some drills you can incorporate into your training.

Small Box, No Rotation
The first exercise you should practice is a simple square. You don't need to use yaw or rotate your drone. Just pitch forward, roll left, pitch back, and roll right so you get a basic sense for your controller.

Reversed Orientation
Next, you can reverse your orientation. Turn the drone 180 degrees so the camera is facing you. Pitch back, roll right, pitch forward, and roll left. This is going to help you understand the common problems and nuances of flying with an inverted orientation.

Large Box, Banked Turns
Next, increase the size of the square, and rotate your turns. Essentially, you're always going straight, but you're rotating left, left, left, at each corner all the way around the square so you get a feel for how to bank your turns.[1]

Figure Eights
Following the path of an "8" parallel to the ground will help you master the art of banking your turns and maintaining elevation as you turn. This is far more difficult than a box pattern. You should master the box pattern before attempting this one.

FPV Flight
FPV flight means you're flying with first-person view only. In a straight line, go from one end of your flying field to the other, without looking up at your drone. The goal here is to focus on flying the drone only through the first-person view. After flying back and forth in a straight line successfully, try flying the perimeter of the park, keeping your drone or your camera view with the edge of the park in the very middle of your framing, and always maintaining that. This will demonstrate the difficulty of keeping a long straight shot, but you'll also learn to trust the drone and fly through FPV.

Below you will find some graphics that illustrate what we just covered, with some more difficult maneuvers included. After getting familiar with the easier drills, progress to these and see how you do. Remember, it might take weeks (or months) before you feel truly comfortable with these exercises.

Be patient. It takes time. You will crash.

But with each pass, you'll get better, and better, and better. Eventually, you'll be able to fly like a pro and capture amazing footage.

And remember: it's worth the effort since that is ultimately what will separate you from other pilots.

Good luck and get after it!

---

[1] If you can bank your turns smoothly, you're likely a very good pilot. This is also how traditional manned-aircraft pilots determine whether a pilot is good or not.

FLIGHT DRILL #1

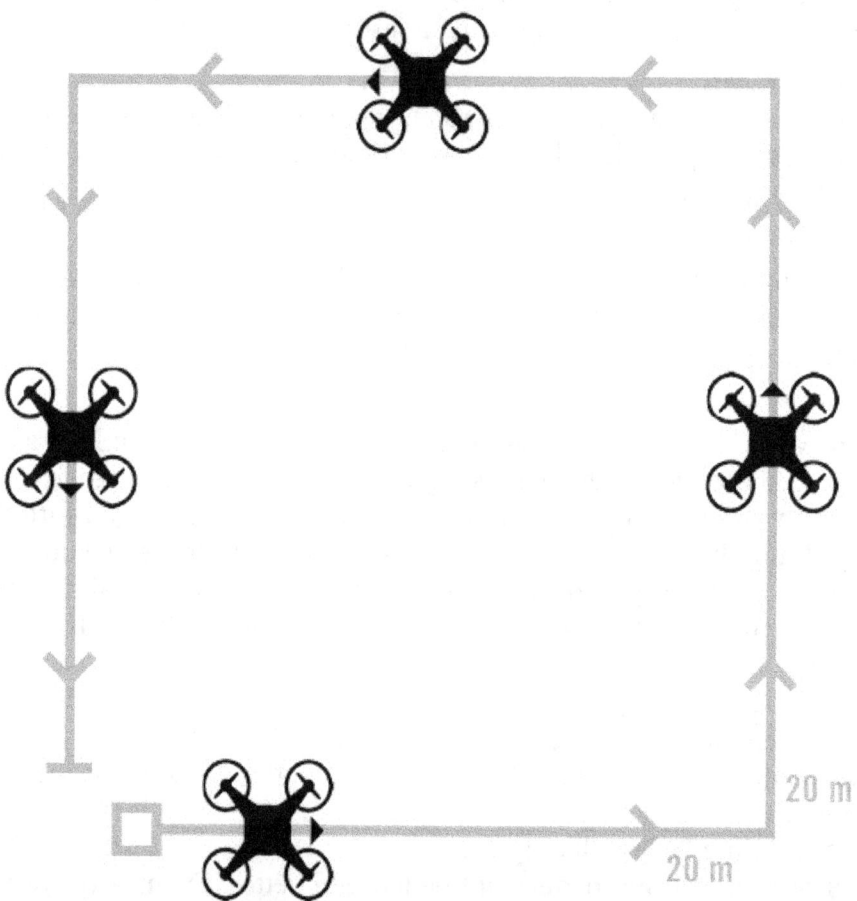

1. Fly the highlighted route.
2. There is a 60 second time limit.
3. You have a 3 meter grace area.

FLIGHT DRILL #2

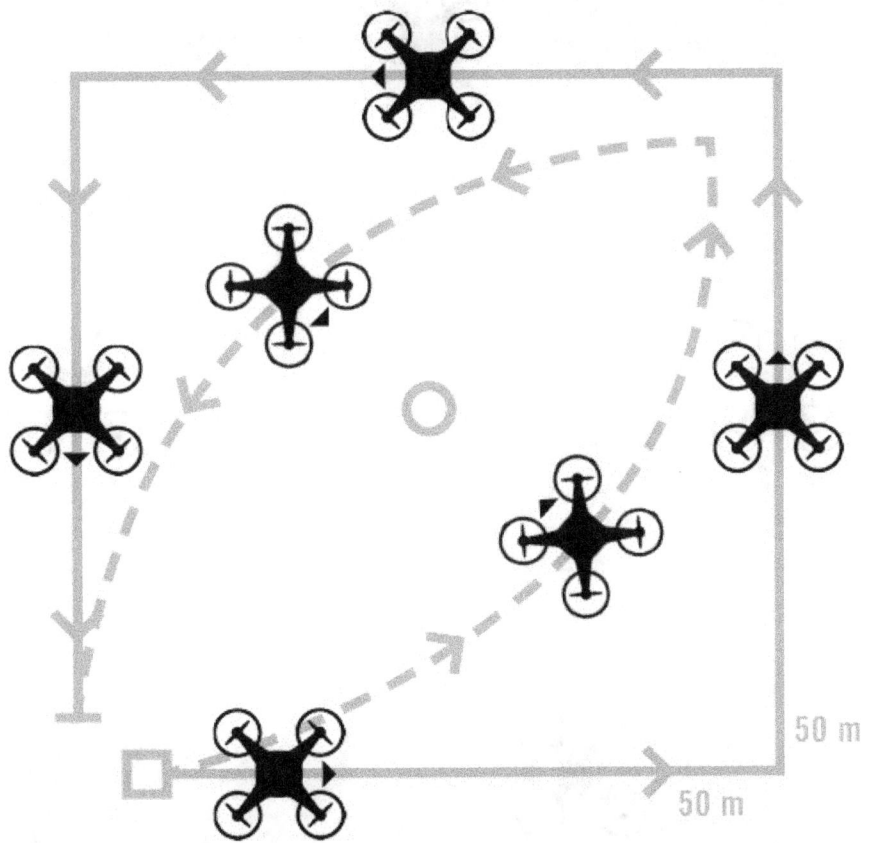

1. Fly the highlighted route.
2. There is a 2 minute time limit.
3. You have a 3 meter grace area.
4. Path 2 must be a complete 180° pan around the center object, keeping the subject in the camera frame.

FLIGHT DRILL #3

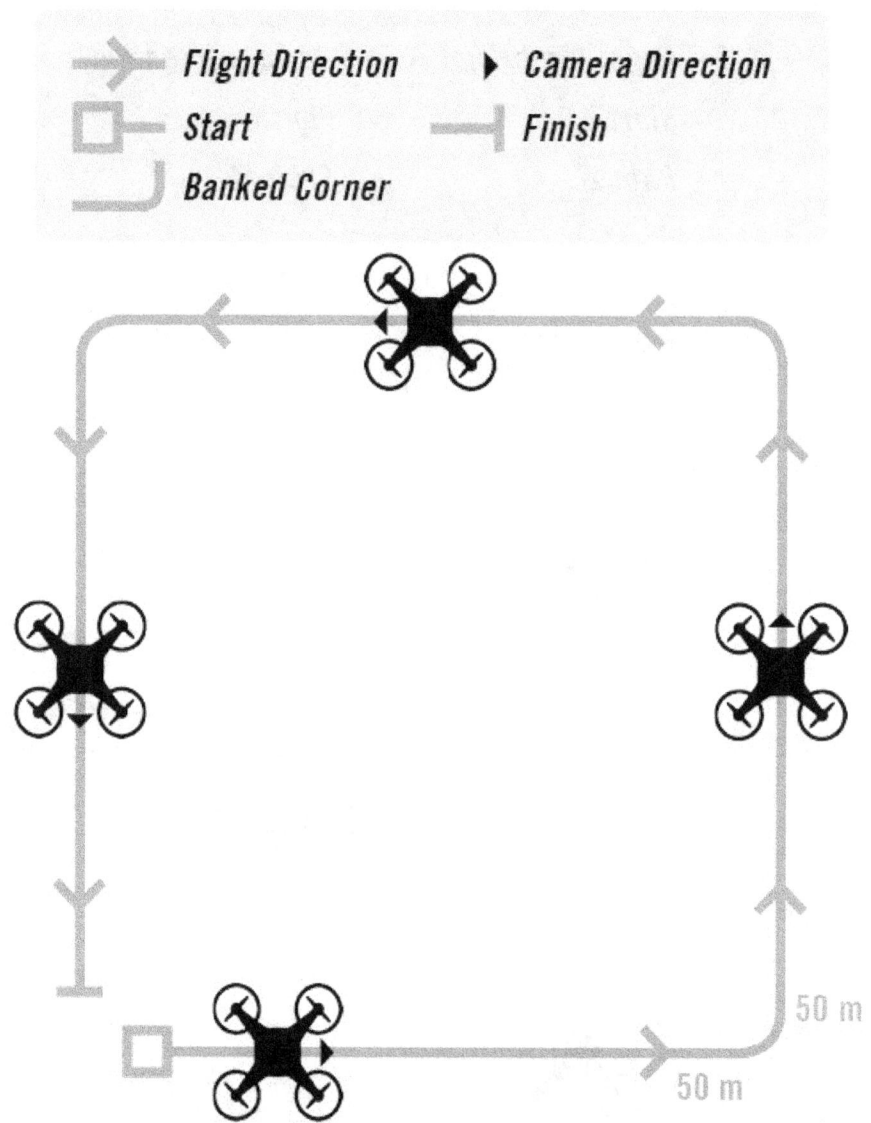

1. Fly the highlighted route, this time banking your turns, which means yawing at the same angle you roll the aircraft. This is a complex movement.
2. Maintain 8m/s minimum velocity.
3. There is a 60 second time limit.
4. Regulate your altititude to 10 m AGL.
5. You have a 2 meter grace area.

FLIGHT DRILL #4

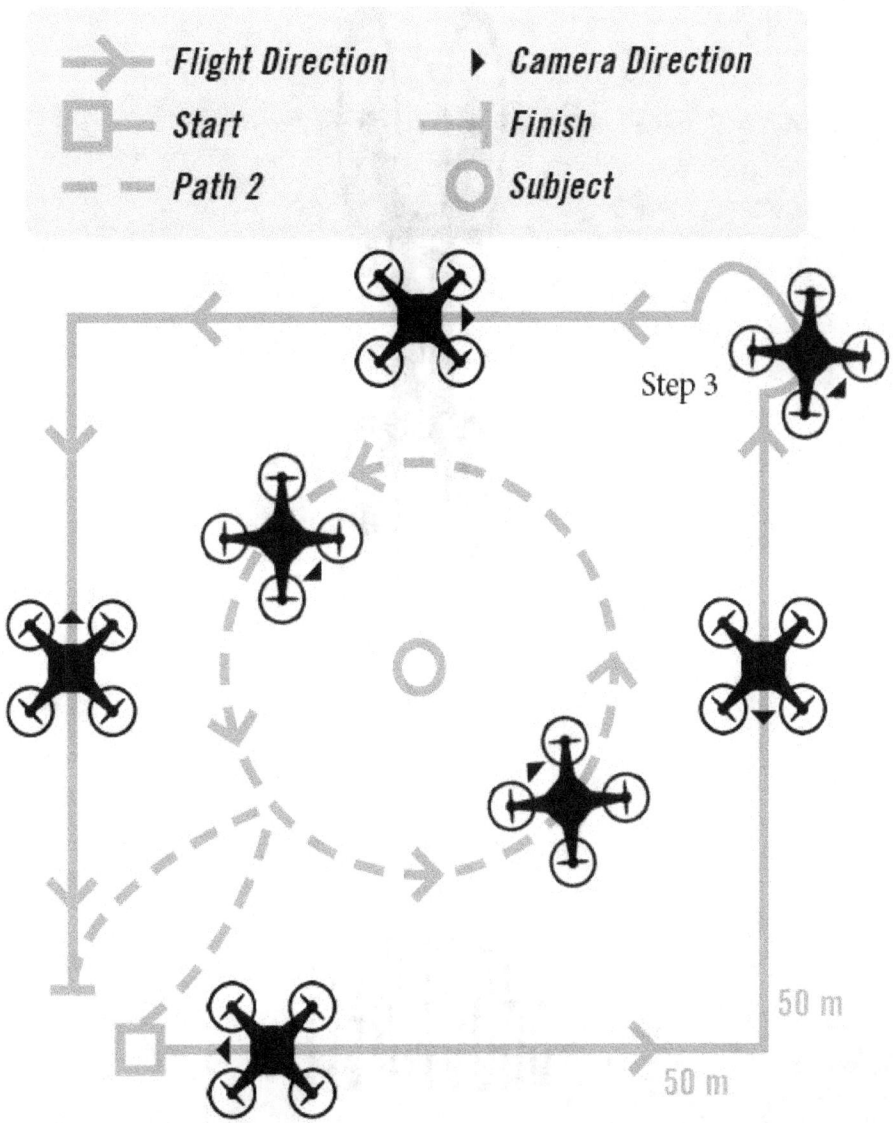

1. Fly the highlighted route *in reverse*, with the camera facing you. This will help you practice obtaining footage in reverse, eliminating the fish-eye effect on a GoPro.
2. There is a 2 minute time limit.
3. Practice turning to the outside of each corner in the flight path, while still maintaining a smooth pan. Practice your 180° pans.
4. Path 2 must be a complete 360° pan around the center object, keeping the subject in the camera frame.

If you're flying a drone, there's a good chance you'll be using it to capture photos or video. This is one of the biggest use cases we see. If you plan to use your drone for something else, you can consider skipping this chapter and the next. That said, we think it's very useful information.

When it comes to shooting good content, planning, prep, and equipment is key. When shooting video, you should adjust your gain and your exposed settings to slow the drone down, especially the yaw. (Remember, yaw is the rotational movement.) If your yaw is too fast, the footage will appear choppy.

OUR VIDEOGRAPHER KIT
Here's our typical inventory for doing a film or photography project.

- Go Professional case "GPC case" (dual case, to hold two drones)
- Inspire 1 and Phantom 4 drones (We always keep the Phantom 4 for a backup. It's also great for flying indoors or through obstacles.)
- 8 Inspire 1 TB48 and 4 P4 batteries
- Polar Pro kit of 6 neutral density and polarizing filters
- Flysight monitor (used for FPV or director feed)
- Extra cables and batteries for the Flysight monitor
- Live-streaming cables
- Extra remote (Live-stream/camera operator)
- Lens cleaning kit
- 3 sets of extra props

Let's talk about various scenarios where videography and photography can be used.

REAL ESTATE

For real-estate projects, we recommend using the Osmo camera. It's the world's smallest stabilized camera. It's essentially the Inspire 1 camera flipped upside down and attached to a gimbal on a stick. You can control the Osmo using an app or a joystick. It's very user-friendly.

Shooting indoors is obviously important for real-estate shoots, and we've found the Osmo to be the most effective camera for this type of work. Other accessories that might be useful to add to your Osmo setup include a suction-cup mount, a tripod, and a dolly or skateboard slider.

For real estate (and any project, really), you should map out your flight plan. Think about what you want to capture, and then walk through the motions and the flight path in your head. You can even sketch this out or list it out on paper. This is essentially *storyboarding*, and we recommend adding it to your workflow as a preliminary step before flying.

It's important to understand that each video has a different style. If you're shooting real estate, your shots should be 4k, 30 frames per second, because the speed of the shot isn't that important. Those settings will allow you to get very high-resolution footage, which you can then downgrade to 1080p in your final cut.

It's also important to think about your audience. For example, in extreme sports, your shots can probably be a little faster. In real estate, the experience should be smooth and calm.

Make sure you get a tour from the realtor and talk to her about how she prefers the house to be shown. If you aren't aware of her typical walkthrough sequence, she'll likely be unhappy with however you choose to do it. The realtor probably always follows a certain flow of walking through the house, whether it's through the foyer into the dining room, or through the foyer into the living room, and so on. We always have the realtor walk us through the house so we can understand the chronological order of what's important to her, and also what's important or unique about the house itself.

One of the biggest issues we see is the failure to obtain a private-property release. These private-property releases are standard in the videography industry, whether you're shooting a movie, a feature film, network television, and so on. You always need private-property permission. Many realtors don't require or ask for a private-property release. But what happens when the FAA asks for it, and you have no documentation? You just violated the terms under which your exemption allows you to fly.

That's why a friend of ours, Jason Bache, and our cofounder, Paul, created an application called Legal Flyer. Legal Flyer is the fastest and most convenient way to get private property permission as well as flight permission. It's like your flight permission slip to be able to fly on the property. It covers everyone who wants to fly.

What if someone calls the police and says you have no authority to fly and that you're spying on people? A property permission release is your get-out-of-jail-free card that says, "I have permission to film here. I'm filming for a realtor." Normally, the police will not have a problem as long as you have some documentation.

After obtaining the private-property permission slip, you need to make sure the house has been completely dusted. It should be completely clean, and the lights should be on. If you're shooting the exterior, the interior lights should still be on so it looks welcoming. We also recommend bringing an extra LED light or an LED kit light. Sometimes to make the shots look as good as possible, you need extra lighting.

Problems to Avoid

Here are some things to watch out for or consider when doing real-estate shoots:

Pets: Don't fly near animals. A lot of people leave their animals out in the yard when you're shooting their home. You should avoid that. Tell your client to take their pets somewhere else for the day.

Obstacles: There are a lot of obstacles inside a home. Ideally, you should have a spotter.

Equipment: Don't fly anything bigger than a Phantom inside a home. If you try to use a bigger model, the prop wash will be so bad that you won't be able to control your movements effectively.

Training Ground

Flying and shooting techniques for real estate are honestly quite simple, which is why we consider real estate the low-hanging fruit for anyone who wants to start earning money with their drone. The nature of real estate will force you to focus on slowing your movements down. It gives you a fixed subject to film. It also gives you a great introduction to lighting and how it affects your shots. If you're not familiar with videography, shooting real estate will teach you composition theory, lighting theory, and how to make cinematic movements without getting yaw or rotation in the video. It's an ideal training ground to learn how to fly.

WEDDINGS

Weddings are one of the most difficult events to shoot, but they can also be extremely lucrative. For prep, you should have your basic kit with you, as well as a shot list. Remember, your shots should tell a story. Show up early before anyone else arrives so you can shoot the landscape, get footage for transitions, and establish the overall beauty of the environment and the venue.

Remember, you're not making an action sports video, so you should use a slow frame rate. We recommend 4k, 30 frames per second. This will produce smooth, crisp shots.

- Typical shots include the following:
- The bride walking down the aisle
- Everyone arriving (maybe an aerial time lapse of the place filling up as the sun is setting)
- The first kiss (or "I do")
- The first dance
- Party scenes

Always respect the wishes of the bride and groom and their families. If you try to capture the bride and groom saying, "I do," people might not be able to hear because of the "buzz" sound of the drone in the background. We recommend testing it out during the rehearsal to make sure everyone's satisfied and comfortable with however you're planning on using the drone, especially during the ceremony.

It's common for people to request a long selfie-pullout at weddings. Everyone's having a good time. They're jumping up and down. Then you reverse your pitch and increase the elevation to showcase the awe-inspiring venue. This is a great shot, and we recommend it. But remember, you need a competitive advantage to build a real business. Don't forget to add in some of your own unique shots and ideas!

Problems to Avoid

Here are some things to avoid or consider during wedding shoots:

Make sure you understand what the bride and groom expect. For example, you shouldn't fly the drone during the ceremony if they're concerned about the sound interfering with the overall ambience.

Set up your gear far way away from the center of entertainment. You don't want anything interfering with the guests.

Don't fly inside if people are present. We've seen a videographer fly his Phantom 3 inside a conference center with three hundred people in the room, directly above their heads. If you remember Flying Ethics 101, you know that's a big no-no.

EXTREME SPORTS

Extreme sports are considerably different than weddings and real estate. The biggest thing to remember with extreme sports is that you're shooting an event. So you need to keep your focus on the action.

Basic Prep

Before filming at a sports event, do the following to prepare.

1. *Turn off Wi-Fi.* A friend of ours was shooting a golfing event. His contract mentioned no one was allowed to broadcast live media while he was in flight. His client didn't follow the rules, and it interfered with his drone's signal, causing it to crash into the turf of the golf course. His drone was worth $57,000. Luckily, the contract was well written, so the client had to pay for the damages.
2. *Plan your flight paths.* Another aspect to keep in mind is your flight path. For example, if you're shooting a track event, you might want to capture a shot of the runner's feet. For that type of shot, you'd need to get very low to the ground, and relatively close to the runners. You'd need to specify a "no-walking zone" to make sure you could fly your drone without hurting anyone. Some coordinators won't allow this, so you would need to inquire about it beforehand. This is why planning ahead is so important.
3. *Prepare based on your battery life cycle.* For extreme sports, or any event you can't "pause," you need to consider your battery life cycle. Bring enough batteries to continually shoot throughout the day. Be sure to factor in the temperature and altitude, which could reduce battery duration.
4. *Use two-way radios.* For any major sporting event, you should also use a two-way radio with a headset to communicate with the production house. Sometimes the event coordinator will provide these for you. If not, you should buy your own.
5. *Plan for speed effects.* It's common to use effects in postproduction for sports footage. For

example, *speed-ramp* shots are popular. This is when the footage goes from normal speed to a faster speed, and then back to normal or slow. Because of this, we recommend shooting 4K at 30 frames per second. Slow motion is hard at 30 frames per second. So if your client also asks for slow motion, you should shoot 1080p at 120 frames per second, and we're sure hoping to see 4k, 60 for ultimate flexibility soon (if not already by the time you're reading this).

6. *Fly low.* Just as with real estate, you should fly low. Sports footage is always best when you can get as up close and personal as possible. If you're far away, the action feels far away, and therefore less exciting. You should speak with talent as much as possible beforehand to let them know you'll be flying close. At bigger events, you might not get that opportunity, but you should always try. It's best to prepare the subject and give him some warning that it might feel as if the drone is very close to him. But reassure him that you'd never put him in harm's way, and you'll make sure the drone is always an acceptable distance away.

Problems to Avoid

Extreme sports is one of the most difficult categories of flying, mainly because you can't plan for what will happen. You have to be able to take great shots in the moment and react to the talent. The best you can do is study the talent if they take any practice runs (for surfing or snowboarding, for example). Your shot is only as good as what the talent is doing inside the frame.

Remember to map out your flight path before the event. Otherwise, there's a good chance you'll run into an obstacle, or fail to capture the shots in the moment.

Watch out for signal strength. For example, if you're shooting a wake-surfing event and the boat travels a mile out, you could lose your signal, and the drone would then fly back to you.

Be wary of distractions. Drones are still a novelty to some people, and you'll find people coming up to you and asking questions about it. Ignore them. If you're at the location with a client, you need to stay focused on the event. The worst possible outcome is missing a shot because you're answering random questions from onlookers. In fact, it's best to partition off the area you'll be flying from.

Be sure to check your shutter speeds and your other camera settings. If you're shooting outdoors, we recommend ND 16 with polarizing filter by Polar Pro. It provides great depth of color and slows down your shutter speed for a nice motion blur.

Watch out for obstacles and any other crew members at the event. Sometimes there are multiple film crews.

RESORTS

Drone videography has a cyclical nature, so resorts and vacation destinations can be great seasonal clients for you. Because there are both winter and summer resorts, this will also give you more constant work throughout the winter months, which is typically the slowest season for videographers.

You can look for winter resorts online. There are popular destinations on both coasts. Colorado is also a great place to look. You should search for these jobs in the fall. You can shoot for winter resort communities, timeshares, rental communities, and so on. You can also travel south to shoot in the winter months. For example, there are usually opportunities in places like Mexico or the Bahamas, even in the winter months.

Depending on the client and the goals, you may need to bring talent into a shoot for a vacation resort. For example, you might want to show a couple walking along the beach, or a family relaxing in their hotel room or at the pool. When you plan your shoot, speak with the client to determine an overall plan for the type of footage and whether or not there will be a human element. This is different from the other categories we've discussed so far, which either have no human element (real estate) or already include people (weddings and sports).

If you're traveling to a destination, remember to carry your batteries onto the plane. You can check the drone. Also make sure you have a private-property permission slip, using the Legal Flyer app.

When you're shooting resorts, continuity editing is recommended. This involves taking a wide shot, medium shot, and close-up shot for each area. It's important to get big, wide reveals, but you also need to showcase the beautiful sidewalk, the plants and landscaping on the property, and all the other small details. By taking all three types of shots, you'll ensure a nice array of footage when you start editing in postproduction.

For resorts, you can usually shoot 4k at 30 frames per second. This will allow you to speed up the footage, but not slow it down. It will also allow you to crop one particular region of the image, and if you output the video to 1080p, you won't lose any resolution. When you are shooting 4k, you're literally shooting four 1080p videos at once, allowing you to selectively crop and choose what you want to show. We find slow motion is seldom used at resorts. That said, you should still speak with your client about it during your prep meeting.

Problems to Avoid

People don't like to be filmed when they're on vacation. When you're shooting resorts, you'll likely be doing it early in the mornings when no one is around. If you see people, you need to speak with them first and get permission to shoot with them in the shot. Otherwise, you need to shoot somewhere else, wait for them to leave, or see if they'd be willing to move. If people are recognizable in your footage, you could potentially be sued (although it's rare).

Any time you fly in another country, you should also research the drone law in that region.

IN SUMMARY

To summarize this chapter, we recommend real estate for novices. It's the easiest type of content to shoot. It will allow you to practice your flying techniques without any human subjects. Resorts are similar, although you might start using human subjects for certain projects. Weddings are a step up in difficulty and will prepare you for the most challenging type of drone projects, such as extreme sports. Once you have some beautiful footage, the next part of the process is editing.

EDITING VIDEO AND PHOTOS

If you're using your drone to deliver videos or photos to a client, the editing process is paramount. Besides flying your drone to capture the actual content, it's the most important skill to master. We'll talk about editing photos first. Then we'll cover video, which is a little more complicated.

PHOTO EDITING
There are several different editing software options. We recommend Lightroom for general workflow and Photoshop for deeper edits. Both Lightroom and Photoshop are produced by Adobe. Photoshop now allows you to pay monthly, which is a nice alternative to paying a large sum up front. Capture One is another editing software, although it's quite pricey and doesn't

offer too much beyond Photoshop's set of features.

With Lightroom, you can organize and manipulate multiple photos at once. For example, you can add metadata to all the photos in a given set, which saves time. You can also adjust presets. For example, you might notice every photo appears too dark. In that case, you could increase the exposure settings in Lightroom with a few clicks, which would lighten all the photos in the set. From there, you can export the images to a folder on your computer (we recommend exporting as either JPEG or PNG files) and edit them further in Photoshop individually.

There are some basic elements to keep in mind when editing photos, including the following:

- Lighting
- Contrast
- Lens corrections

Lighting
Let's use the example of a new property—a tall building in a busy city. The property owner wants to showcase the building with a set of aerial photos. Using editing software, you can lighten the building, and then darken everything else around it. This will bring focus to the building and cause the surrounding buildings to fade into the background.

Contrast
Without contrast, we can't distinguish shapes or colors. If the subject of your image is bleeding together with the rest of the content, it essentially disappears. Adjust the contrast to make the image pop and to differentiate all the various objects within the frame.

Lens Corrections
Many GoPro cameras will create a fish-eye effect, meaning the horizon line will become distorted and curved. Sometimes people like this effect, but you can also make basic lens corrections to correct it if it's not desired. Normally, this fish-eye effect is not desired.

Practice
Adjusting the lighting and the contrast, as well as making lens corrections, will improve with practice. There's no set rule for how to do it. As you edit more content, you'll train your eye to spot issues that need improvement. From there, it's just a guess-and-check process to create the best output possible. Drone U offers several photo editing courses taught by Vic Moss, who has won multiple HDR photo competitions. We, of course, highly recommend these courses if you'll be working with photography!

VIDEO EDITING
Imagine a video with a single, flowing shot. The drone is flying us over the water, and you can see the horizon. There's soothing, melodic music in the background. It's as if you're a bird, enjoying an afternoon excursion.

Now imagine another video. This time, the shots are quick, cutting from one scene to the next. You see a skateboard up close, and then a bunch of tricks in sequence. The shots are jerky but stylized, almost as if to match the haphazard nature of riding a skateboard. Upbeat music is playing along with the video, and each shot changes with the beat of the music. You can't see the rider, so there's an element of mystery.

The two videos we've just described create entirely different moods, which are evoked through editing. Postproduction editing turns raw footage into an experience. The combination of music and artful visuals can trigger emotions unlike any other medium. Let's go over the basic tools and steps for turning raw footage into amazing art.

Software

The two basic software programs for video editing are Final Cut Pro X (or FCPx) and Adobe Premier Pro. If you're working in broadcast news, you might use AVID Media Composer. Adobe Premier is considered the industry standard, although we find Mac users prefer Final Cut Pro. Final Cut Pro is a little easier to learn, especially if you're accustomed to Macs.

There are other programs you'll use in conjunction with these core products, depending on which one you choose. For example, if you want to create three-dimensional animations and you're using Adobe Premier, you'll use another program called After Effects to create the three-dimensional animation. If you're using Final Cut Pro, you'll instead use a program called Motion.

The Story

When you're shooting video, you should have an idea of the story you're trying to tell. For example, let's say you're planning to shoot a wake-surfing video. The goal is to showcase the people, the tricks, and the memories they had together. As you shoot the event, let the story in your head guide your focus.

Organizing Footage

After shooting your video, you should go back and watch your footage. Open a spreadsheet and record time stamps of the best shots—the ones you plan to include in the final cut. Then specify whether the shot is *A-roll* or *B-roll*. *A-roll* footage is content that will take priority and includes both video and sound. *B-roll* footage is content you'll show with just music in the background, or with a voiceover, but the footage itself has no usable audio to it. In other words, *B-roll* is all about the video because any audio is going to be dubbed over whatever it is you're shooting.

Once you've organized the footage into shots for the final cut, you can visualize the entire video as a whole. Again, it's important to think about the overall goals of the piece. For example, in this case, we're shooting video for a wake-surfing event. That means we shouldn't be including shots of just the boat, since wake-surfing is the primary focus.

Once you've gathered your shots and made sure you have the proper focus, you can begin editing. Open your editing program, and import all the clips you've selected. While your footage is uploading (which can take a long time), search for music to accompany your video.

Music

Music is critical because it usually dictates the frequency of your shots. If you have music in your video (which is very common for most client work), the visual content should align with the music. If the music has a distinct beat, for example, each shot should change on the beat. Once the music is laid down and your clips have uploaded, you can start editing each shot to make sure your cuts are as precise as possible. This will create a more polished finished product.

Transitions

In the past, transitions were used frequently. A transition is an effect that happens between two shots. The most common transition effect is a fade to black. In more modern videos, transitions are used less often and most cuts are *jump cuts*, meaning there are no effects between shots. We recommend using transitions sparingly, but they can certainly add to the overall production quality if implemented well. If you choose to use them, you should always add transitions while you're compiling your shots. If you wait to add them until the end, it will ruin the alignment with the beat of the music. Remember to lay down the music first, since it dictates the composition of the visuals.

Clipping and Flow

Once you've added your shots to the timeline, go back and watch the video in its entirety to get a feel for the overall flow. You may find you want to move shots around, or use different content in certain sections. Once your shots are flowing nicely together, zoom in on your timeline to get as precise as possible with your clipping. For each cut, you should try to find the exact millisecond when the beat hits, and then trim your shots to cut at that exact moment.

Color-Grading

Finally, you need to *color-grade* your footage. The goal with color-grading is to make the colors as accurate and vibrant as possible. Or, if you're trying to create a certain mood, you may want to color the footage stylistically. For example, if the video is supposed to feel somber, you could desaturate the footage to make it more gray. Or if the footage is supposed to feel psychedelic, you could amp up the saturation.

Text, Graphics, and Exporting

The last step is to add any final text or graphics, such as the client's logo. Then you can export the video and watch it again to make sure it exported correctly. You can also add metadata when you export the video, such as a video description and keywords. This can improve the SEO (search engine optimization) of the video if it's made available online.

Common Problems

Here are five problems to watch out for when editing video.

1. *Frame rate discrepancies*: When editing footage, make sure the frame rate setting within your editing software matches the frame rate setting of your footage. For example, in the movie industry, the standard frame rate is 23.97 (don't ask us why!). If you then switch gears and shoot some footage for another project at 30 frames per second, but forget to change your editing software settings, you'll end up with *clipping*. This means the raw footage will be clipped by the editing software based on the discrepancy of the frame rate settings.

    There's one exception when differing frame rates are okay. If you're planning to use slow motion, you should film at a high frame rate and then set your project settings to be a divisible factor of that rate. For example, you could shoot at 120 fps, and set your project settings to 30 fps. This would create a slow-motion effect that displays the footage four times slower than the original live speed. It's important to use multiples to keep the footage smooth. For instance, you wouldn't want to use an editing setting of 50 fps in this case, since 120 isn't a multiple of 50.
2. *Poor color-grading*: You should always color-grade your footage. It's by far the most difficult part of video editing, but your final product will look amateur without it. This isn't necessarily something you need to do yourself. You could outsource it. We recommend Upwork.com for finding freelancers.
3. *Lazy editing*: Editing is challenging because it often requires removing fairly good content to improve the project as a whole. It's common to include average shots or to have sloppy clipping. When you're editing, you should always be thinking, "Can I take anything else away to make this better?" It's important to include only the best shots, and only the *best*

parts of the best shots. We recommend going through your project two or three times to polish your jump cuts. This is an art, not a science.

4. *Inconsistent syncing with music*: The previous step (editing shots) is even more challenging when adding music into the equation. It's important to match your shots with the music. You have to find the right combination of amazing content, but *also* match the content with the flow of the melody and the beat. In some cases, you may need to extend a shot or clip it short in order to align it with the music. Aligning with the music takes priority over cutting the shot at the ideal place.

5. *Exporting issues*: You need to make sure you export to the correct file type and video codec. For example, if you're shooting for broadcast media, you should be shooting at 60 fps (at a minimum), and your output file should use the H222 codec. If you export the file with an H264 codec, the file size will be smaller, but the quality will suffer. We won't be covering codecs and exporting options in detail, because it's outside the scope of this book, but you can do a quick Google search to figure out which export settings are best for your particular type of work.

IN SUMMARY

As we stated at the beginning of this chapter, editing is arguably the most important part of the production process, outside of capturing the actual footage. You should invest considerable time and energy into practicing this critical skill if you plan to take photos or video with your drone. There are, of course, other sensors and tools you can use with a drone besides a camera. In the next chapter, we'll talk about those applications.

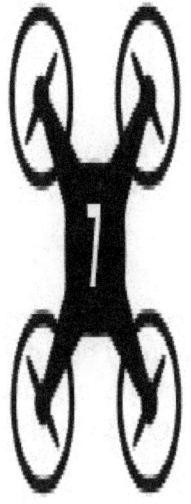

SENSORS:
BEYOND PHOTOGRAPHY AND VIDEOGRAPHY

Even though the emergence of drones has created a proliferation of video- and photography-related businesses, drones can be used in other capacities as well. Remember, a drone is technically defined as an unmanned aerial vehicle with imaging sensors. The most common sensor is an optical camera, which allows us to capture photos and video. But other sensors can take your drone beyond these traditional mediums. In this chapter, we'll define the main sensors currently being integrated with drones and provide examples of how they might be applied to a business. We've touched on these before, but this section includes more detail.

The five major sensors are these:

1. Electro Optical (EO)
2. Thermal (Infrared)
3. LIDAR
4. Multispectral
5. Hyperspectral

OPTICAL SENSORS

Optical cameras capture traditional photos and video. This is the most common sensor and the easiest to understand. Any standard camera that captures photos or videos would fall into this category.

INFRARED SENSORS

Infrared sensors, also referred to as *thermal cameras*, detect radiation. To clarify a common misconception, they don't detect temperature. They detect the actual radiation emitted from heat. Infrared cameras can be used for various purposes, including surveillance and security, livestock detection, water source identification, emergency response, and search and rescue.

Thermal cameras are useful because almost all living things emit heat. This means infrared technology can be used as a tracking device. If someone goes hiking and gets stuck in the mountains without food or water, it would be difficult to find them with the naked eye. It could take days, or even weeks. With a thermal infrared sensor, however, you could fly a drone over fifty square acres within an hour and quickly identify the person by his or her body heat.

Search and rescue doesn't just apply to humans either. In Colorado, a horse named Houdini (how perfect!) went missing. His owners reported the stray horse to the police. They looked for Houdini for four days, to no avail. Luckily, Kerry, a friend of Drone U, lived nearby. He had a thermal camera attached to his drone. He surveyed the area and found Houdini within twenty minutes.

Infrared sensors can also be helpful in law-enforcement pursuits. If someone stole a car, crashed, and then ran into a dense forest on foot, it would be difficult for officers on the ground, or even in a helicopter, to spot the target. But a drone with infrared sensors could find the subject immediately.

Thermal cameras are also good for detecting livestock within a given area. Let's say a hunting lodge wanted to know how much game was on their property. They could fly their drone with a thermal camera to map out every animal in real time, and then relay that information to their guests.

LIDAR SENSORS

LIDAR stands for "Light Detection and Ranging." It's a remote sensing method that uses light in the form of a pulsated laser to measure ranges or variable distances to the earth.

This means a LIDAR sensor can produce incredibly accurate orthomosaic and topographical maps that include precise measurements of the ground and its elevation. In other words, it can display each ridge, crest, and valley of the Earth's terrain with incredible precision.[1] This has valuable applications in the fields of construction, architecture, and civil engineering.

MULTISPECTRAL SENSORS

The term *multispectral* generally refers to multiple bands of light that are represented in colors. In multispectral sensors, each band of light is acquired using a special sensor that is designed to only look at specific waves of light. This sensor has many applications, but we see it used most frequently in the agriculture industry.

For example, a multispectral camera can measure water quality and vegetation density. It's so accurate that it can literally index plants on a farm. Just as Google Maps can identify each home along a street, a multispectral camera can identify each individual plant and give it a unique identifier.

With this level of detailed reporting, farmers can improve the efficiency of their resource allocation. For instance, after a heavy rainfall, they might only need to water a small section of their farm that received less water, instead of their entire set of crops.

Multispectral cameras can also measure the *health* of plants, by scanning for certain bands of light emitted or absorbed by diseases. The camera can search for levels of carbon, phosphorus, nitrogen, and so on. By tracking the density of these elements, farmers can easily see which plants are sick and which plants are healthy.

With such hyperspecific tracking capabilities, drones can also prevent the excessive use of herbicides and pesticides, which could eventually reduce the rate of chemically induced cancer.

HYPERSPECTRAL SENSORS

Hyperspectral sensors can see individual narrow bands of light. They can distinguish between bands separated by 10–20 nanometers. An image might include hundreds of thousands of unique bands of light, but this camera can identify a single band with distinct properties. If you know the reflectivity and light-absorbance properties of a specific compound, you can set a hyperspectral camera to look for that specific compound.

This can be helpful in a number of situations. For example, there's a mineral compound called *humate* that helps plants grow with less water. Humates are commonly found in the southwestern United States. Using a hyperspectral camera, farmers can survey their land to figure out which areas contain the highest density of humates. They can then strategically plant certain crops in those areas to increase their yield.

THINGS TO CONSIDER

If you're planning to use any of these sensors for your business, the first consideration is, of course, learning to fly. You can't expect to use these sensors effectively unless you're a skilled pilot.

Secondly, you should be aware of the various licenses you might need depending on the work you're doing. If you expect to sell orthomosaic maps, for example, many businesses will require a surveyor's license to interpret your maps. The actual regulations around surveying are still hazy, but it's always safer to obtain official credentials if possible.

We know a pilot who made a topographical map for a construction site using volumetric measuring software. During the foundation stage of the site, he was fined $75,000 for interpreting maps without a surveyor's license. To avoid similar fines in your own business, you can seek out surveying companies who will approve your work in the absence of a license. These companies usually charge a small fee in exchange for their stamp of approval. (It's essentially like an accounting firm doing your taxes. They take on the liability by representing you.)

It's also important to understand the limitations of your hardware and software. If you're using a standard consumer drone and camera, you might not be able to capture images with enough accuracy for your client. For example, we once mapped a building with a GoPro drone. The images weren't detailed enough, so we eventually had to give the project to another operator with more sophisticated equipment.

As you build your drone business, you'll quickly learn which sensors are best for you. In the next chapter, we'll cover all the other areas of your business besides the drone itself.

[1] In terms of outputting map data, we recommend using DroneDeploy. DroneDeploy will store all your content in the cloud, so it renders much faster. There's another program called Pix4D, but it requires a dedicated machine with a massive amount of memory and storage.

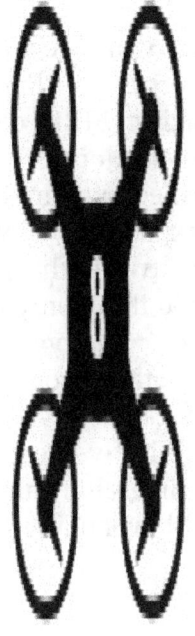

SELL WELL

One of the purposes of this book is to help you, as a drone pilot, understand what it means to become a successful business person. We often see skilled pilots who fail to understand the basic business principles that will turn their skills into profit. This is why so many talented drone operators go bankrupt. It's the same reason restaurants, doctor's offices, and law firms fail. Perfecting your trade is only one small slice of the business pie.

    Let's think about the franchise model for a moment. One reason franchises are so successful is that the owners essentially give you a business in a box. They tell you how to market the product. They give you advice for handling human-resources issues. They tell you how to find a good lease and obtain insurance. By providing support in these areas, the business is more likely to generate profits, which leads to sustainability over the long term.

In the drone world, this infrastructure is in the earliest stages of development. We hope to take a big step forward by explaining the basic building blocks in this book.

FIND YOUR NICHE

As we've discussed in previous chapters, your niche will determine how your organization is run, as well as the equipment and resources you'll need. For example, if you're performing methane inspections, you'll need a specific FLIR camera, like the Alpha 65. Or, if you're working in videography with a focus on vacation resorts, you'll need to understand the cyclical nature of the industry to optimize your project pipeline.

Choosing a niche is relatively self-explanatory. We recommend following your passions, versus chasing a concept that appears lucrative in the short term. Because the drone market is so young, there are many opportunities. If you think only about the hottest business categories as of today, you're limiting yourself. The market will continue to mature, so we think it's best to take a long-term approach. If you work on something you love, you'll be more likely to stick with it, even through the inevitable adversity you'll face as your business grows.

Don't think about where you want to be in five years. Instead, consider the problem you want to solve. Then take one small step at a time along the path to solving that problem. If you're willing to put in the time and effort, you'll eventually put yourself in position to compete as one of the industry's top leaders.

What Are You Already Good At?

Play to your strengths. If you have a math or engineering background, consider learning more about drone-based businesses that rely on mapping software. Mapping often applies to civil engineering, biochemical engineering, and agriculture. You could also abstract this further and build software to integrate with all drones. For example, you could marry various sensors together. On the other hand, if you're more of a creative person, consider learning about aerial photography and videography, which has applications for events, real estate, film, and entertainment.

As you think through various business opportunities, you should also consider the barriers to entry. For instance, getting started with mapping is more difficult than getting started in real estate. It might make sense to do some simple real-estate or aerial photography projects, knowing your ultimate end goal is to start a mapping business. This is one potential strategy for building your skills in a beginner's market before jumping into a tougher industry.

To continue this line of thinking, you also have to consider the maturity of the market. Some markets are further along and more accepting of drones than others. In real estate, many property managers are already accustomed to using drones and integrating them into their business, either directly or through contractors. Mapping is a much more difficult sector to break into, because, beyond the more expensive equipment required, the industry is still hesitant about using drones versus the traditional alternatives.

Gas and oil inspections are other areas where companies are more hesitant to engage with drone operators. Many of these businesses are unsure of the legal ramifications and regulations, so it can be difficult to find work. As you weigh potential business opportunities, you must consider the conditions of the broader market and how that could affect your likelihood of failure or success.

Below are two lists we've separated into "less difficult" and "more difficult." We've chosen these titles deliberately to make sure you understand that no path will ever be easy or without hurdles to overcome. Additionally, these markets may change over time as new drone regulations and laws are passed, so take the lists with a grain of salt.

Less Difficult

- Aerial photography
- Real-estate photography
- Real-estate videography
- Weddings
- Construction photos or videos (no mapping)

More Difficult

- Vacation marketing videography
- Pipeline inspections
- Home inspections
- Agricultural inspections (plant or animal tracking)
- Surveillance
- Movies
- Action sports videography

ACCESSIBILITY

Certain industries might be more accessible to you based on your geographic location. For example, if you live near an oil patch, you might consider starting a business relating to the oil industry. Or if you live by farms, you could explore agriculture. If you live near Aspen, Colorado, action sports could be an option. If you live in California, you could consider film and entertainment. Conversely, if you *know* you're interested in a particular location-dependent industry, consider moving to the geographic location that best serves that industry.

REGULATORY LANDSCAPE

You should investigate the regulatory environment where you live. Some states are more proactive in passing legislation that restricts what drone operators can and cannot do. It's very dynamic. Before you invest too much time exploring a given niche you're planning to exploit, make sure you'll be able to run your business legally from wherever you reside.

USE YOUR NETWORK

With any business, it's vital to plug into your own network and the professional network surrounding your industry. We observe many drone operators who get so focused on their product and the inner workings of their businesses that they forget to build relationships with partners and customers.

INCORPORATION AND REGISTRATION

We're not lawyers and we're not offering legal advice, but we still think it's important for you to understand the basic makeup of a business from the legal standpoint.

An initial step for all businesses is to incorporate as an official corporate entity. This allows you to decouple the liability of the company from your own personal liability. It also means you'll owe business taxes based on the financial standing of the business, which is completely separate from your personal taxes.

We strongly recommend creating a corporate structure for your business. Many people start off as sole proprietors, but that leaves you liable if the company goes bankrupt, which means the government could seek restitution in the form of your personal assets (your savings and/or property). You would also be personally liable for any claims made against you by a client.

There are a variety of corporate structures. We recommend incorporating as either an LLC or an S Corporation. You could also consider a C Corporation, although it's probably unnecessary at the early stages. Again, corporate structures are outside the scope of this book, and you should research them on your own, but the key takeaway is to avoid being a sole proprietor. This will significantly reduce the risk of your suffering any personal liability should your company fail.

After setting up a corporate entity, you'll need acquire a tax ID numbers, from the IRS, for federal and state taxes. Next, you should set up or hire someone to handle your accounting. Accounting is fairly easy to outsource, and there are now software options or software/human hybrid solutions that can assist with your accounting needs. We recommend Quickbooks Online by Intuit. Bench is another accounting company that helps small start-ups offload their accounting and bookkeeping tasks.

A word of advice: Even if you outsource this, you should still learn about it and have a basic understanding of your *P&L* (profit and loss) or "income" statement, your *balance sheet*, and your *statement of cash flows*. These three documents will form the backbone of your business from the financial perspective. Without a clear understanding of how money is flowing in and out of the business, you could abruptly find yourself in financial trouble.

PAYMENTS AND INSURANCE

You'll also need a system for letting people pay you. Of course, you can accept cash or check, but clients often prefer to make payments by credit card. To set this up, we recommend using Square. Square allows you to take credit card payments in a matter of minutes, without the hassle of creating a merchant account with payment processors.

Another important piece of your business infrastructure is insurance. This is especially important in the case of a drone business. Insurance will give both you and your clients peace of mind. In fact, some companies won't do business with you unless you're insured. Regardless, since the new drone law doesn't require it, insurance is quickly becoming a competitive advantage.

Insurance also protects you from crippling financial burdens. We've seen people try to use their homeowners insurance or renters insurance to cover their drone. That's not what we mean. You need specific insurance for your drone to cover any damages that could occur from operating it. Homeowners or renters insurance would only help you if your drone was stolen.

You should have general liability insurance for your business, but you should also have aviation-based insurance specifically for your drone. The first group to offer this was Transport Risk Management. They're based out of Colorado, and they've written thousands of policies, but they have a long application process. Global Aerospace, Costello Aviation, and Traveler's Insurance are a few other options that provide aviation-based insurance.

We recommend at least $1 million in liability insurance. You should also have hull insurance (which just means equipment protection), people insurance, and property insurance. Hull insurance covers the cost to replace your drone if you crash it. People insurance covers medical expenses if you crash your drone into a person. And property insurance covers the cost if you damage someone's private property.

Pro Tip: Getting a course certificate from Drone U can reduce insurance costs. In many cases, if you provide verification that you received professional flight training, the insurance provider will lower your premiums.

CONTRACTS

You should draft a formal proposal for every business engagement. The proposal will lay out the scope of the work, the terms, and the pricing for the deliverable. To create solid contracts, you'll need legal advice. This is not something you should do on your own, nor should you copy boilerplate language from the Internet. You should find a lawyer who has experience in contract law. The contracts don't necessarily need to be long. They can often be executed on a single page if done well. You should also always keep a copy of every contract for yourself, either in digital or hard-copy form.

There are certain conditions relating to drones that a typical contract lawyer wouldn't know to include. So you may need to use a contract lawyer *and* an aviation lawyer.

We mentioned we know a drone pilot who was operating a golf event. During the event, someone at the golf course emitted a radio signal, which caused the drone to crash into the fairway. The fairway was damaged and so was the drone, which was worth approximately $57,000. Fortunately, the pilot had a good aviation lawyer who had specified in the contract that no radio signals could be emitted while the drone was in flight. Because of that clause, the pilot wasn't liable for the damages, so the client had to pay for both the damage to the golf course and the drone.

There are some basic forms you can access at Drone U, like a private-property release form. You can also access basic forms on iTunes and Google Play for various photography and videography apps. That said, we still recommend using a lawyer for your master proposal contracts. You can also do a simple Google search for "aviation lawyers" or "contract lawyers" to find other options.

PAYMENT AND OWNERSHIP TERMS

You should negotiate payment and ownership terms up front, and incorporate them into your proposal contract. Never do work before the contracts are signed. We've seen numerous businesses get suckered into doing "spec work," only to find out the client never intended to pay any money. We recommend creating a portfolio so you can use it as a defense against doing spec work. If someone isn't sure about the final product she'll receive, simply point her to your previous work as an example. If this isn't enough for her to feel comfortable, you probably shouldn't work together.

We also recommend securing a portion of the payment up front before work begins, to make sure the client is reliable. It's typical to require 50% of the total project cost up front and 50% upon successful completion, but you can choose any amount or percentage you like. If the client feels uncomfortable with your initial terms, you can always tweak them and negotiate on a case-by-case basis.

MARKETING

A major aspect of your business (that exists outside the product itself) is your marketing. You have to represent yourself as a professional and communicate why your product or service is better, or preferred, over the competition. Stories help create and sell your brand. How can you build a story around your product and then communicate that story to your customers?

In today's world, the story typically starts online. First and foremost, you should have a website. For website creation, we recommend SquareSpace. Weebly, Wix, and WordPress are other options. After setting up a website, you can advertise it on social media.

Think about marketing as *building relationships*, versus *advertising your product*. No one wants to be interrupted by a salesperson when they're walking down the street. But if you reach people casually through social media channels and then slowly build a rapport with them, they'll likely eventually see the value in what you're selling.

Every business should have a fundamental Internet strategy. Think about where your audience might live. Are they more likely to be on Snapchat, Instagram, Pinterest, or LinkedIn? Or somewhere else? Pick one to three channels to focus on first. We recommend starting with Facebook and a few others. Then set up a system to capture emails when people visit your site. You can store emails with a service like MailChimp. You can set up tools to *collect* emails with services like LeadPages or SumoMe.

If you're in a business that isn't necessarily drone-specific, use the novelty and efficiency of drones as part of your core selling point in your marketing message. For example, if your company focuses on phone tower inspections, you could highlight the fact that you use drones for inspections, while your competitors use trucks. You can tell the story of how your business uses cutting-edge technology to make the process safer and more efficient. You can talk about how quickly your drone can inspect the towers, with the same (if not better) accuracy as a person inspecting them from a truck. This creates a compelling story around your product. If you do this well, it won't feel like marketing.

HOW TO MARKET YOUR COMPANY LIKE A PRO

Marketing is about communication. Your goal is to explain why customers need your service. You shouldn't think of this as "selling," but rather "teaching." Customers are far more likely to listen to you if they feel you're offering authentic information, versus just fishing for dollars.

Demo Reels

One of the first steps in this process is to show examples of your work, or the finished product customers can expect. If you're in the field of photography or videography, a *demo reel* is the best way to showcase your talent. It will explain your service better than words, while also highlighting your unique talents.

A demo reel is a short video, usually two to five minutes long, depending on how much work you've done in the past, that showcases your best work and the various types of content you offer. It usually includes short clips of your previous projects, stitched together into a "reel," or flow of shots. A music track typically plays in the background to tie the visuals together.

After seeing videos or photos you've produced in the past, customers will be able to visualize the output for their specific project. You can use your demo reel on your website or in live presentations with prospective clients. It serves as both sales/marketing collateral *and* high-quality web content. We'd recommend displaying your demo reel directly on your homepage. If you work across various industries, you can show clips from all the industries you've served, which is a good demonstration of your versatility.

Because your reel is so indicative of the final deliverables you're able to produce, you should invest a significant amount of time and money into it. We recommend getting your reel edited professionally versus trying to do it yourself. A professionally edited reel will have a completely different effect than raw footage. The professional edit will be color-graded and speed-ramped, with polished cuts and music. It's your chance to create the best first impression possible.

Digital Branding

In today's Internet-connected world, it's important to establish your own personal brand, or *self-brand*. Building up your brand can generate leads that eventually convert into sales for your business.

The easiest way to strengthen your personal brand is through social media platforms. Facebook, Instagram, Pinterest, and Twitter are all great places to start. We'd also recommend investigating Snapchat, LinkedIn, and Reddit. Find one or two channels you like, and commit to them. Self-branding isn't about getting direct sales. It's about building awareness and trust. You should develop authentic content and share valuable material related to your business. To create leads, include a *soft-sell*. This could be a link to your business site in your Twitter bio. It isn't a direct call to action, but if your content is good, a percentage of visitors will click through and land on your site.

Each network is different. For example, Facebook is great for building relationships. It's very targeted, so you can set up a business page and then target people who, for very specific reasons, might be interested in what you have to offer. In contrast, Twitter isn't very good for building relationships, but it's great for building credibility. If you can attract a large number of followers, prospective clients who view your Twitter page will assume you have some clout and that you're an established company. While this may not necessarily be true, a large number of followers still creates that perception. As you build your social media footprint, keep these nuances in mind. You likely won't be able to build a strong presence on every single service. But if you find one to three that work well for you, you can create a powerful digital brand that serves as the backbone for your marketing strategy. At Drone U, about 80% of our advertising budget goes to Facebook. We've found that to be our strongest channel.

There may be costs associated with maintaining a social media presence, for both your personal and business brand. For example, if you build a Facebook page for your business and start posting content, only 6% to 8% of the people who liked your page will actually receive the posts in their feeds. You can improve this conversion by copying the post to your personal account. We've found posting to a personal account typically reaches 30% to 40% of your friend list. Unfortunately, a personal account probably won't yield nearly as many leads, since those people are your friends and not necessarily your target customers. If you want to increase the spread of your content to targeted customers, you can set up advertising campaigns, or pay to boost your posts, which means Facebook will show them to more people. The ROI on this can be hard to measure, but we recommend testing it with a relatively small budget. To gauge whether or not social media campaigns are bringing customers into your sales funnel, send customers a survey and ask them where they found you. Typeform, SurveyMonkey, and Wufoo are all simple and free surveying tools we recommend.

CASH FLOW IN RELATION TO MARKETING

It's easy to lose track of your marketing costs. Our simple and admittedly obvious advice is to plan your marketing budget, track it, and stick to it.

We recommend setting up surveys and tracking systems so you can measure the performance of your various marketing channels. Then you can allocate more budget to the best channels over time and turn off the ineffective ones. Most lead-generation tools have a system for tracking leads. Be sure to learn about these options and use them whenever you can.

You can also look for free ways to advertise your business. Social media is again arguably the best platform for free advertising and marketing.

Because drones are such a hot topic, public relations is another valuable tool. You can use both good news and negative stories about drones to build a local brand and correct misconceptions.

You should assume a percentage of your revenue will always be reinvested in the company in the form of marketing. By tracking your other expenses, you can determine what percentage can be allocated to marketing while still maintaining positive cash flow, month over month. Find a percentage that works for your particular business. Maybe it's 5%. Or maybe it's 25%. Then optimize the ROI for that budget. Also, keep in mind that the percentage allocated to marketing (as well as the absolute number) will change over time. In the early stages of your company, it might be a very small number. That's okay. Getting your feet wet will pay dividends later. Over time, you can increase the budget, which will then theoretically accelerate growth.

HOW TO AVOID COMMON MISTAKES IN MARKETING

Test, Test, Test

The biggest mistake we see in the area of marketing is failure to test. We see businesses creating ad campaigns on Facebook, but they only create a single ad. They should be creating multiple versions of the ad and determining which messaging works best. People also run ads without testing their effectiveness. Marketing for the sake of marketing is dangerous. You need to ensure the dollars spent on the front end are generating revenue on the back end.

Define Your Audience, Then Find Them

You shouldn't assume one marketing channel will always be the best channel. We've run campaigns on Facebook that have worked beautifully, and others that have tanked. Usually, when the campaign doesn't work, it's because we tried to reach a specific audience in the wrong place. For example, Snapchat caters to a younger and more casual audience, while LinkedIn caters to an older and more professional audience. If you're trying to attract a young, casual demographic, advertise on Snapchat and avoid LinkedIn.

Seek Referrals

Another common mistake is failing to seek referrals. In the world of drones, referrals might be the number-one most effective marketing strategy. Word-of-mouth is still the strongest form of advertising. If you're working with real-estate agents, the best way to get business from other real-estate agents is to ask existing clients to tell their friends. In a new industry like drones, there's a lot of doubt from the consumer side. If you work with a client and he's thrilled at your output, take advantage of that relationship. Ask the client to spread the word, or to recommend other similar clients who might be interested in your services. If you've built trust with the client, he'll usually have no problem becoming an advocate for your business.

You should be intentional with this. Deliberately ask for the referrals. Don't just hope they'll come. You should be actively asking your most satisfied clients, "Do you know anybody who might be interested in my services? How can I connect with them?"

You need to have a system, or a routine, for doing this. It doesn't have to be complicated. Simply identifying a specific point in the project life cycle where you ask for referrals can be enough. If you don't set up a system or integrate this into your plan, you'll forget. It can be as simple as including language about referrals along with a thank-you email after you've received final payment. In a culture dominated by social media, it's easy to forget that referrals are often the most effective strategy for generating leads.

PRICING EFFECTIVELY

The first step in pricing your work is to consider the costs of producing it. You'll likely need equipment directly related to the drone, plus other peripheral equipment (for example, a car if you need to drive to a location). You also might need to pay contractors for editing or other postproduction work. On an income statement, these expenses are typically called COGS, or Cost of Goods Sold (especially if the costs are consistently the same across projects). The project-related costs are the baseline for pricing your final product.

Some freelancers and small businesses get confused at this step. They think they should just calculate their costs and then mark up the price by a certain percentage to reach a final number.

This is okay, but there's not much logic to it. How do you determine the markup?

One way is to look at comparables, meaning other similar products and services. If the rest of the market is charging a certain price for your type of service, you can safely assume that's the price the market will bear. To stay competitive, you should select a price in that range (assuming you're confident it will cover your costs and provide some profit).

There's a final step that's often ignored: Use common sense and charge what you think you're worth, based on the previous analysis we've just described. For example, if you see the market is offering a range of $1,000–$2,000 for the type of service you're offering, it doesn't mean you need to stay in that range. If you think your product is better than the competition, you can try charging more. Or, if you've created some proprietary system that allows you to produce the same quality output for a lower cost, you can consider lowering your price and undercutting your competition, knowing you'll attract more customers while maintaining competitive margins.

It's always easier to charge more up front and then decrease your pricing over the long term. For that reason, we recommend starting at a higher price and then lowering it until you see a comfortable conversion on sales. That said, your pricing strategy should change if you're completely new to whatever business you're starting. In that case, you should set prices a little *lower* than what you actually hope to charge in the future. It's not realistic to command premium prices if you have little or no experience in the field. You may also want to offer a quick example deliverable for free. This is the *only* time we recommend doing this. It should not be part of your ongoing strategy, but sometimes it's necessary in order to get your first few clients.

Single-Use and Multiuse Licenses

Photography and video content shouldn't always be priced solely based on the product. The intended use also affects price. If the content is used for one purpose, it can be sold as a single license. However, if the client expects to use it for multiple purposes or resell it to third parties, it should be priced as a multiuse or exclusive license. The difference in price in these cases is significant.

If you sell the exclusive rights to the content for multiple uses, you can mark up the price anywhere from five to ten times the original price. To give a concrete example, if you were to create a promotional video for a vacation marketing company, you might charge $2,000 for the video. This would be a single-use license. If, however, the marketing company planned to sell the video to small vacation rental companies as marketing material, they would need to purchase an exclusive license. This exclusive license might cost anywhere from $10,000 to $20,0000, *for the same video.* It's therefore very important to lay out the intended use of the video and write language into the proposal contract that would allow you to sue the client if the content was used for multiple purposes without your consent.

Multiclient Discounts

Your pricing strategy might also change if you plan on selling your deliverable to multiple parties for a single project. For example, if you're taking marketing photos of a construction site after the site has been built, you could charge the construction firm. But you could also charge the architect if he wants to use the material for his own branding purposes. And finally, you could charge the real-estate firm in charge of marketing and leasing the property.

In this case, you could draft up a multiclient discount to entice all three parties to participate in the deal. This is a win-win situation because your total price increases but the unit price decreases for each buyer.

To illustrate this with actual numbers, you might charge $1,000 for a single license, but $750 per license for more than two licenses (a 25% discount off the original price). If only two of the three buyers participate, you receive $2,000. (Both buyers pay $1,000). But if all three buyers participate, you receive $2,250. (Each buyer pays $750). In the latter scenario, you've done no extra work, but you receive a higher payout. And for the buyers, they all receive the deliverable for a cheaper price. Everybody wins.

Don't Be Afraid of Losing Business

If you try to please everyone, you'll please no one. We often see inexperienced business owners coming into the drone market and trying to please every client. This is a bad long-term approach. It's not scalable. If you're getting every job you're bidding on, you've priced yourself too low. You'll get every deal, but your margins won't be high enough. You'll be completely overbooked but won't earn enough to pay the bills over the long haul. There's a big difference between profitable and busy. You want to be profitable. If you're not profitable, being busy doesn't help. On the other hand, if you price yourself too high, you won't close enough deals.

You need to find the sweet spot. The price should be aligned with the quality of the final product, consistent with comparable services in the market, with a high enough margin to cover your costs. If your product is high quality, based on the competition, charge more for it. If you're offering a quick and dirty solution that's less professional, charge less. But always keep an eye on your costs and your cash flow.

Common Mistakes in Pricing

Here are some common mistakes in pricing:

- Underestimating your value
- Deliberately pricing yourself too low
- Trying to please everyone
- Not understanding costs
- Failing to invest in perceived value (i.e., not spending time and money to create a high-quality demo reel)
- Spending unnecessarily on equipment and infrastructure before learning to fly
- Not researching comparables to price effectively

As we've mentioned, it's best to start with a small, cheap drone to learn how to fly. Then incrementally upgrade your equipment to bigger drones as necessary. Be realistic with your skill in terms of your pricing, but also realize that the market is nascent, so you *do* have some leverage as a seller.

SCALING YOUR BUSINESS

To grow your business effectively, you'll need to offload certain tasks. You can't expect to do everything yourself. The first task we recommend outsourcing is video editing. While you should learn the basics of editing, you can easily outsource this task to a talented editor overseas for a reasonable price. The price of an editor overseas will often be a fifth of the price you'd pay for someone in the United States.

You can also outsource your graphics, both for video content and for your general brand and marketing material on your website.

There's really only one aspect of the business you can't outsource, and that's flying your drone. Remember, even though you can outsource most of the work, you still have to manage your cash flow. You may not have enough cash on hand to outsource everything initially. This is an art and not a science. You need to free up as much time as possible so you can fly your drone and make money. But you also need enough money to pay contractors so you can free up that time. The best approach is to do this in increments. Initially you'll be doing most of the work yourself. Once you have some cash flow, you might be able to outsource one task in your business. After closing a few more deals, you might be able to outsource one more task, and so on.

Don't spend money you don't have. Often times, clients might not pay you for forty-five to ninety days after the project is complete. Depending on your cash flow, this can be a huge problem, so err on the side of caution.

IT'S A BUSINESS, SO TREAT IT LIKE ONE

We did an interview with an analytics company on the future economic growth of the drone industry. They believe we'll see a massive influx of drone-based businesses in 2016 to 2017 as more common-sense and business-friendly regulations are passed by Congress. They also estimate that between 2017 and 2019, we'll see about 60% of those businesses go bankrupt because of acquisitions or an inability to compete.

There are a lot of great drone pilots, but very few of them are also exceptional business people. If you're expecting to start a drone business and turn your passion into profit, you really have to spend time working on your business. You need to develop the right systems, routines, and workflows so you can scale. That's one of the reasons we wrote this book and created Drone U. We hope it allows you to start your business, take it to the next level, and *stay* in business.

THE ELEPHANT IN THE ROOM: THE FAA

PAST STATE OF GRAY

Depending on who you ask, drones were first used in the United States sometime between the 1950s and 1960s. The confusion lies in how we define a drone. The terminology continues to evolve. Common acronyms include UAV (unmanned aerial vehicle) and RPA (remotely piloted aircraft). But is a drone really an aircraft? Regardless of how we choose to define them, the regulations surrounding drones have been hazy from the very beginning.

In the past, we lived in a state of gray. A bunch of *advisory circulars*, or policy statements, have been released over the past several years. But policy statements are merely suggestions. They're interpretations of how regulatory agencies may react to written law. According to

Douglas Marshall, a professor of aviation at the University of North Dakota, "By issuing a policy statement, an agency simply lets the public know its current enforcement or adjudicatory approach."[1] Simply put, the policy statements are explanatory, rather than prescriptive.

To make matters worse, these documents are typically vague and unclear. And the agencies have the authority to change how they react to policy statements at any given time, without judicial review.

In Canada and Mexico, pilots have been flying drones for years. In 2014, there were 1,500 registered drone pilots in Canada. The United States, by comparison, had fifty. President Barack Obama has echoed the sentiments of Congressmen Davis and others who believe drones can play a positive role in our society but need better regulation. In a statement released on CNN in early 2015, Obama said, "There are incredibly useful functions that these drones can play. In terms of farmers who are managing crops and conservationists who want to take direct stock of wildlife, there are a whole range of things we can do with drones, but we have no regulatory structure at all for it."

Many have argued whether or not the FAA really has authority to regulate drone commerce at all. Congress created the Federal Aviation Administration (FAA) in 1958. In 1967, they moved the agency to the Department of Transportation, which made it part of the presidential cabinet. Congress gave the FAA jurisdiction to regulate navigable airspace. The term *navigable airspace* has been a point of contention with drone pilots and operators. The FAA has said, "Navigable airspace is defined as airspace above minimum safe altitudes of flight prescribed by regulations."

But what are the minimum safe altitudes? *14 CFR 91.119 B* says that "the minimum safe altitudes are 1,000 feet above the highest obstacle in uncongested areas," and that "airplanes can operate at an altitude of 500 feet above the ground, but have to be operated up, over, and around a 500 foot bubble for any person, vessel, vehicle, or structure."

What about the airspace from your house to the 500-foot level? Does a homeowner have rights to that airspace? In most cases, yes. But it really depends on the regulations of your particular state, which can contradict the regulations of the FAA. Typically, the space above your house up to about 500 feet would be considered Class G airspace, which is defined as uncontrolled airspace. This means air traffic control "has no authority or responsibility to control air traffic" in those areas.[2]

Loose rules and guidelines have made drone operation far from easy, but thankfully, there's progress. August 29, 2016, will be remembered as the official start date of the modern drone industry in the United States. On that day, the FAA released Part 107: small UAS (unmanned aircraft systems) rules.

With the ruling, the barrier to entry for commercially operated drones was lowered significantly. It means pilots no longer need a full pilot license. Instead, a remote pilot license is sufficient. Initial estimates show that within ten years, the drone industry will generate more than $82 billion for the US economy, creating more than 100,000 new jobs.

Here are two of the most significant advancements from the ruling:

1. *UAV operators*: Before the ruling, only fully licensed private or commercial pilots were able to operate UAVs commercially. This created a major problem for most companies because they didn't have access to a licensed pilot (for budgetary reasons, or otherwise). The new rule allows for specially trained UAS operators to fly drones commercially. The certificate will only cost about $150. This makes incorporating drones into your business far more economical than ever before.

2. *Operational limitations*: The new rules allow commercial UAVs to fly from zero to 400 feet above ground level, at speeds less than 100 miles per hour. Drones may fly closer than 500 feet to a building, just as long as they don't fly over people. Drones may only be used during daylight, while maintaining a visual line of sight at all times. The regulations also limit the aircraft from being heavier than fifty-five pounds. Drone operators will be unable to fly in restricted airspace (such as near airports) without a specific waiver, known normally as a COA. COAs last for two years, but you can use them to petition parts of the 107 to allow operations from moving vehicles or in tight airspace, and to allow news companies to fly drones over large crowds. While these regulations may sound somewhat strict, we still see it as a step in the right direction since the rules are clear.

OBTAINING A LICENSE

So how does someone get his or her 107 license?

Basic Qualifications:

1. At least sixteen years of age
2. Physically and mentally able to safely operate a small UAS

Requirements if you don't have a pilot's license:

1. Pass the initial aeronautical knowledge exam. This can be done at a local computer-assisted testing service (CATS) center. Get your study material from Drone U!
2. Fill out and submit the FAA Form 8710-13 for a remote pilot certificate using the electronic FAA Integrated Airman Certificate and/or Rating Application system (IACRA).
3. That's it. You'll receive your certificate in the mail.

Requirements if you already have a pilot's license:

1. Complete the online training course "Part 107 small unmanned aircraft systems (sUAS) ALC-451," available on the FAA FAASTeam website.
2. Fill out and submit the FAA Form 8710-13 for a remote pilot certificate using the electronic FAA Integrated Airman Certificate and/or Rating Application system (IACRA).
3. That's it. You'll receive your certificate in the mail.

You should study for these exams/courses. We've developed study material in conjunction with multiple CFIs (FAA certified flight instructors).

Taking a test to get your license is only the first step. Here are the next few steps to take immediately after you pass your exam.

1. Search for nearby airports. File for a COA in that airspace so you can fly there on request. Schedule a meeting with the airport manager to discuss the COA and set up an LOA (letter of agreement). The letter of agreement states the terms in which you both mutually agree you can fly.
2. If you plan on using your drone for videography, file a COA to fly out of a moving vehicle.

That way, if you're ever asked to do a long sequence for a movie or a commercial, you can do it from your car without any issues.
3. If you're flying thermal cameras, operating for search and rescue, or inspecting commercial roofing systems, file a COA for operations at night.
4. If you're doing power-line, gas-line, pipeline, or distribution-line operations, file a COA for BVLOS (beyond visual line of sight operations) ops.

Remember, COAs only last two years. We recommend turning your COAs into editable PDFs so you can edit them quickly and easily and then refile.

WHERE SHOULD I NOT FLY?
All of these regulations are enough to make your head spin. Unfortunately, it's the world we live in. Our best advice is to err on the side of caution to avoid further scrutiny or complications. If you're running a drone-related business, the last thing you want is an enforcement action from the FAA or a local agency. Here are some general guidelines. (We know we've stated many of these before, but they're worth repeating.)

- Don't fly near airports or helipads.
- Don't fly near hospitals.
- Don't fly near critical infrastructure (bridges, dams, etc.).
- Don't fly near stadiums or TFRs (temporary flight restrictions).
- Don't fly over people in general.
- Don't fly in national parks. The National Park Service released this rule in 2014.
- Don't fly near military bases (or government-owned property, such as the White House).

This list might seem to be common sense, but it's easy to forget when you have a drone in your hands. Before launching it into the sky, look at a map. Make sure you're not too close to anything that might lead to trouble.

Airports
If you fly within certain distances of an airport, there will be different requirements depending on whether you're flying as a hobbyist or as a commercial operator. The distance "barrier" can vary from airport to airport. Therefore, it is critically important that you check aeronautical maps prior to flying.

For the hobbyist, we recommend AirMap.com. They have a great app as well, so you can quickly check maps on your phone. As a hobbyist pilot, you need to contact the airport tower and notify them that you're in the area. You don't actually need permission to fly in the area, per se. But you still have to let the tower know your location and plans. Be aware that they still can impose limitations on you. For example, they might request that you fly below a certain altitude. You should always comply with their requests, so long as they are reasonable.

For the commercial operator, we recommend using SkyVector.com as your source for aeronautical charts. Unlike the hobbyist, the commercial operator does need permission to fly in the designated area. It's no longer as simple as making the tower aware of your presence. This all changed with the Part 107 drone license requirements. As of the writing of this book, the FAA wants you to go through their online portal to request permission (FAA.gov/UAS/Request_Waiver), not to directly contact the tower. Unfortunately, as is the case with most new processes, this has proven incredibly frustrating and inefficient. We hope the

FAA will take this problem very seriously and make swift adjustments in order to make the system viable, both for commercial pilots and those working in the airport tower. As of right now, the system really is not at all viable for either side. We do still recommend that you follow the system in place and go through the FAA's designated process. However, we also recommend that you actively seek to establish relationships with those working at your local airport towers. Introduce yourself to them, let them know what you do, be patient with them and kind to them, and foster a mutually beneficial long-term working relationship. They need to know that you're working in the area, and you need to be able to get permission in a timely manner. Having good rapport with your local tower operators will ensure this for both parties. It can be a win-win for all involved.

HOW DO I FLY WELL IN THIS REGULATORY ENVIRONMENT?
As stated above, our recommendation is to be cautious and play the game. While most of the regulations are messy, unfounded, and contradictory, they still might affect your ability to fly. If you follow the basic steps to operate your drone legally, you should be able to avoid any serious legal prosecution.

Ideally, you should obtain a 107 Remote Pilot License. Most people pay for a single class for $250 to $500 dollars. However, you can get all of your study material for free as a member of Drone U. After obtaining your license, you'll need to learn how to get airspace approvals and more to maintain the competitive advantage over your competition. Don't forget, you still need to fly well!

The more successful you get, the more you'll have to contend with authorities. Your competition might even call the FAA on you, stating that you're flying commercially without proper authorization and credentials. They'll try to impose restrictions on you. They'll try to get local enforcement officers to question whether you can fly legally or not. The fact is, you need to be educated to respond. These are the realities of participating in the drone industry.

If you have a 107 Remote Pilot License, it'll be easier for you to market your services. It's also a safety net. If the FAA calls you, you can simply present your green license and get back to business. Case closed. Conversation over.

WHAT ROLE SHOULD DRONE OPERATORS PLAY?
We need your help. Drone operators should be privacy advocates. They should be legality educators. They should be safe flight monitors. If you see someone flying over a crowd of people, say something. Explain why it's dangerous and ill-advised. Tell the pilot it could lead to an enforcement action if someone complains, or if the authorities find out.

By educating people and becoming a community advocate, you can help regulate the lies and misconceptions about the industry. A lot of operators are airplane pilots, and they're not actually good *drone* pilots. Many pilots are also young kids, or hobbyists who could care less about the regulations.

Unfortunately, we've witnessed a lot of backstabbing within the drone community as well. In most cases, enforcement actions correlate to a complaint from a Section 333 operator who decided to throw another pilot under the bus. People operating with exemptions are calling the FAA on other non-Section 333 operators in hopes of killing their business. This is bad behavior and sets a poor example for the entire community. We have to be mutually accountable, but we should also be respectful. Let's all navigate this together. We're on the same team, and there's plenty of business to go around.

RULES WE CAN AGREE ON

Certain rules should never be broken. (Look familiar? Repetition of information will ensure you internalize the most important stuff.)

Don't fly higher than 400 feet. The best drone shots are from thirty to fifty feet anyway. There's no reason to fly higher.

Don't fly below the treetops where neighbors might suspect you of invading their privacy.

Stay five miles away from any airport. If you need to fly closer, notify the airport because you never know if there are going to be temporary flight restrictions (TFRs). For example, if a political figure is heading into town, they might close the airspace completely.

- Don't fly near helipads.
- Don't fly over people.
- Don't fly in national parks.
- Don't let the drone out of your direct line of sight. Fly by visual line of sight only.
- Don't fly in urban environments, especially between large buildings. If you fly between two tall buildings, you could have a GPS interference problem.
- Don't fly near national infrastructure such as steel bridges or dams, because the magnetic inference could cause you to lose your drone.

If you follow the safety standards and guidelines of the AMA, you'll be in good shape.

If drone pilots are spying on people, or flying near manned aircraft, or deliberately causing trouble, the industry will continue to regress, and our government will invoke more rules, which is exactly what we want to avoid. The United States is already one of the slowest to develop clear guidelines, rules, and standards for drone operations. The choices we make in the field will affect everyone in the future. So let's be smart about it.

That said, there will undoubtedly be more regulations to follow, as this is a work in progress. But we at least now have steps to follow, and what we've tried to do here for you is give a succinct summary of what you need to do to get a drone license.

In the end, this isn't really complicated: Fly safe! Be a drone advocate, participate in a thriving community, educate yourself, continually look for good training, learn from other like-minded enthusiasts, and help educate your peers. If we stick together and act responsibly, we can move the industry forward.

---

[1] Douglas M. Marshall, ed., *Introduction to Unmanned Aircraft Systems* (Boca Raton, FL: CRC Press, 2011).
[2] Section 14-3 of *The Pilot's Handbook of Aeronautical Knowledge*.

CONCLUSION
BUILD THE DRONE FUTURE

Technology always evolves. It's like a river, constantly flowing. And it can't be stopped. So the question is not whether you believe in drones, but whether or not you will choose to use them to your advantage. Drones aren't just a new piece of technology. They're a new platform. They'll create hundreds of new jobs, change existing industries, and spawn new ones. They represent the next big tidal wave of our development as a species.

    We expect drones to get smarter. Obstacle-avoidance features will continue to be added to the existing hardware, making them easier to fly. That said, learning how to fly manually will still be critically important, as we're learning you can't trust technology. If you run into magnetic interference, or a solar storm, or a wind storm, or your battery is failing, will you know how to fly your drone back to safety without harming anyone? Since drones will do most of the flying themselves in the near future, the majority of pilots will be subpar in terms of their actual flying ability. If you learn to fly manually, you'll have an edge on your competition and be able to produce higher-quality work.

Drones will allow businesses to compete on price because of their efficiency. For example, in the field of cell tower inspections or pipe inspections, drone-based companies will be able to undercut non-drone-based companies by simply doing the work more efficiently and with less liability. This will drive prices down, which is a good thing. With more efficiency comes higher margins and happier customers.

Autonomous drones will enable even greater efficiencies that might be hard to imagine today. For example, packaged delivery may no longer require humans. Amazon might start delivering your packages with drones instead. The industries of engineering, construction, infrastructure, and agriculture, among others, will all be affected.

In fact, because drones will be both easier to fly and cheaper in price, we expect them to flood nearly *every* market. As prices decrease for the consumer, businesses will need to compete along other dimensions. Twenty years ago, a wedding video captured with a drone would cost several thousand dollars. Today, there are numerous freelancers willing to do it for a few hundred bucks. When a market matures, products within that market become commodities. In those conditions, the single leverage point that separates big winners from everyone else is *quality*.

Looking a little further into the future, it's well within the realm of possibility to assume people will use their drones for personal tasks as well. Just as computers now help us perform many day-to-day tasks, drones will do the same. For example, if you forget your wallet at home, you could simply send your drone back to get it (instead of sitting in traffic).

From sensor technology, to drone technology, to drone law—everything is changing rapidly. This isn't a bad thing, though. It means it's a great time to get involved. The wave hasn't yet begun to crest. You can be part of the community that fights for the freedom to fly, for the right to privacy, and for the next economic boom. You can rise with the tide.

For the drone industry to progress, we need new regulations that will allow small drones to be flown in unregulated airspace with limited restrictions. Congress is pressing the FAA to stop stifling the industry, to allow for more commercial applications, and to allow small drones to be more accessible to the general public. We've already seen a massive step forward with law *14 CFR 107*, which allows any pilot to fly a drone upon passing a written test.

Bigger projects will most likely continue to have more stringent "requirements." For example, if you want to use your drone to film on movie sets, the unions will probably still expect you to have a pilot's license and a Section 333 Exemption. However, this doesn't make any sense because according to the FAA you are covered once you've obtained your Part 107 drone license. This is especially true since licensed drone operators will no longer need a special form to work on movie sets; the 107 license is all you need (unless you plan to fly over people). But this is a reality we will have to fight through and try to overcome by humbly and gently educating those we talk to, regardless of industry.

Regardless of where your interests lie, there's plenty of business to go around. We caution operators who contact the regulatory agencies to complain about other drone pilots. That type of behavior is regressive. Instead, everyone should focus on the quality of his or her own work. If the big agencies see bickering and fighting within the community, the regulatory processes will stall even more. But if we support each other, we'll protect our collective right to fly and speed up the creation of new comprehensive laws.

It's absolutely critical for us to become advocates for this industry. If we don't, the ability to use the technology to advance society could be hindered significantly. We have an opportunity to stand up and let our voices be heard. We need to be evangelists.

We've already seen success stories through our work at Drone U. One of our students, Tyson, runs a business to support construction companies. He takes three-dimensional photos of construction sites using drones. He has created a passive, recurring-revenue business by running his company professionally, while keeping things simple. Tyson said of Drone U, "[It was] exactly what I was looking for when I wasn't sure what I was looking for. Their business focuses on what I needed to get *my* business started."

Another student, Dave, said, "A small investment, signing up for Drone U, has been one of my smarter business decisions. Their team and the community has been nothing short of spectacular in terms of knowledge, knowledge transfer, and guidance. Knowledge is power, and this holds especially true for the UAV community in these trying times, as regulations are constantly changing and a general sense of confusion plagues our industry. The Drone U team helped me enlighten my clients on the current regulations and put their mind at ease about the services we provide. I've recommended a subscription to Drone U to all my colleagues."

Another member said, "Drone U offers a comprehensive overview of drone ownership, use, and operation that I have been unable to find online. Even more valuable is the individualized attention you get, including specific answers to questions from experts you trust. I learned a great amount of information and was challenged to put what I learned to use through practice and flight drills. I would recommend Drone U to anyone who wishes to take their drone use to a professional level."

We invite you to join us in the Drone U community, where you can constantly learn, gain a competitive advantage in your business, and turn your passion into profit. Whether you're a new drone pilot or a veteran looking to polish your skills, we're here to help.

We'll show you the tips, tricks, and nuances that will turn your toy into a tool. If you build a drone-based business, you'll realize you can get out of the office, travel, and make money in the process. It's not a bad life. And if your business is more traditional, or you're building a larger organization, there's still a good chance drones could improve your workflow in those scenarios as well.

We hope this book gave you a taste of the possibilities drones present. They will undoubtedly affect your day-to-day life, and society as a whole, whether you choose to build a drone-based business or not. This is a disruptive technology that will transform our entire world. You can stand on the sidelines or get into the game. We hope you'll come play.

If you have any further questions, please visit us online at www.AskDroneU.com, or listen to our podcast, *Ask Drone U*.

There's an unbelievable opportunity in front of you, and the sky is quite literally the limit. Have fun, live the drone life, and fly safe!

www.ingramcontent.com/pod-product-compliance
Lightning Source LLC
Chambersburg PA
CBHW081125080526
44587CB00021B/3754